GERMANY AND
THE REVOLUTION
IN RUSSIA
1915–1918

GERMANY AND THE REVOLUTION IN RUSSIA 1915–1918

*Documents from the Archives
of the
German Foreign Ministry*

EDITED BY

Z. A. B. ZEMAN

LONDON
OXFORD UNIVERSITY PRESS
NEW YORK   TORONTO
1958

Oxford University Press, Amen House, London E.C.4

GLASGOW   NEW YORK   TORONTO   MELBOURNE   WELLINGTON
BOMBAY   CALCUTTA   MADRAS   KARACHI   KUALA LUMPUR
CAPE TOWN   IBADAN   NAIROBI   ACCRA

PRINTED IN GREAT BRITAIN

ACKNOWLEDGEMENTS

THE editor wishes to acknowledge the help of his wife and her patience. Mr. George Katkov was both helpful and interested—this was important. Mr. Dietr Pevsner translated most of the official German into readable English. The Warden and Fellows of St. Antony's College, Oxford, helped to relieve the editor of some of the more onerous tasks connected with producing this volume by a generous grant from the College. The Librarian of the Foreign Office rendered many kind services to the editor. The editor would also like to thank his friends and colleagues who helped him, encouraged him, and bore with him.

London, May 1957

INTRODUCTION

In November 1914 it became clear to Germany's leaders that they had failed to achieve a decisive victory in the first phase of the war. The transformation of the war in the West and in the East into a one-front engagement was, according to Falken-hayn, the Chief of the General Staff, the shortest way to victory.[1] It could be effected only if Germany concluded peace with one of the principal partners of the Entente.

Zimmermann, the Under State Secretary in the Foreign Ministry, concurred with this opinion in a memorandum dated 27 November.[2] He wrote: 'The aim of our policy in this war, conducted with such uncommon sacrifice, must be not only an honourable, but also a lasting peace. In order to achieve this aim I regard it as desirable that a wedge should be driven between our enemies, so that we may conclude an early separate peace with one or the other.' In the subsequent years of the war, to isolate one of the enemy powers and conclude a peace with it was the principal aim of the German foreign policy.

Behind this policy there was a tremendous profusion of activity and confusion of thought. The Foreign Ministry, having lost its peace-time functions, took over its management. The German missions in the neutral countries were the Ministry's busiest outposts. Politicians, journalists, members of noble families, university professors, directors of banking houses, industrialists, cranks, and crooks were involved. Large amounts of money were spent by the government in order to achieve this aim.[3]

France and Russia were the most likely targets for the policy of separate peace. But in Russia, apart from the possibility of concluding peace with the established régime, there was another way open to Germany. This was to give support to the revolutionary movement, to weaken the existing régime not only by military defeats but also by disruptive revolutionary agitation, both nationalist and socialist, and finally to conclude peace with a government dependent upon German good-will.

The Imperial government never made a clear-cut choice

[1] Bethmann-Hollweg's letter to Zimmermann, 19 November 1914 (AS 2769 in WK 2 secr, volume 1). For explanation of archival references see pp. xiii and xiv.
[2] AS 2769 in WK 2 secr, volume 1.
[3] The relevant documents on German peace-feelers in the Great War can be found in the series WK 2 secr and WK 2.

between the two courses of action open to it: from 1915,
throughout the war with Russia, it pursued the policy of support
of the revolutionary socialist movement, especially its left-wing
elements, and the various separatist, nationalist movements,
such as the Finnish and the Ukrainian. At the same time, the
Germans used every opportunity to negotiate with the representatives of the government they were doing their best to
weaken and deprive of its power.[1]

It was Dr. Helphand,[2] alias Parvus, by origin a Russian Jew,
a Social Democrat who attempted to stand above the
Bolshevik–Menshevik controversy, who did much to attract
the attention of the German government to the possibilities of
a revolution in Russia. From the spring of 1915 till November
1917, Helphand played the most important part in Germany's
relations with the Russian revolutionary movement, in spite of
the fact that some socialists distrusted him, and that he may
have been by-passed when the various German agencies
acquired their own contacts. In November 1917 he parted
company with the German government and made an attempt
to pursue an independent policy.[3]

Although the centre of political power had shifted, at the
outbreak of the war, from Berlin to the seat of the Highest Army
Command, it was the Foreign Ministry, and not the General
Staff, who played the leading role in the policy of support of
the revolutionary movement. It was pursued with the approval,
and, in broad outline, with the knowledge of the highest military levels, and in co-operation with the Political Section of the
Deputy General Staff in Berlin.[4] The Political Section, first
under Nadolny and later with Hülsen at its head, played an
important part in the implementation of this policy. But the
initiative came, most of the time, from the Foreign Ministry.

The support of the left wing of the Russian revolutionary
movement, political and financial, was the policy of the Foreign
Ministry throughout the war. It was initiated while Jagow
was the State Secretary, and Zimmermann the Under State

[1] See editorial note, p. 23, and footnote 3, document No. 90.
[2] No biography on this interesting subject exists. Deutscher, in his biography
of Trotsky, *The Prophet Armed* (London, 1954, pp. 99 et seq.), discusses
Helphand's relations and influence on Trotsky. K. Haenisch, the German
Social Democrat journalist, wrote a short pamphlet, entitled *Parvus* (Berlin,
1925).
[3] See editorial note, p. 72.
[4] von Moltke, the predecessor of Falkenhayn in the General Staff, was the head
of the Deputy General Staff office in Berlin.

Secretary in the Auswärtiges Amt; it was carried on, more intensively, by Zimmermann after Jagow's resignation and later by Kühlmann, who saw its consummation and decline in the final stages of the war.

It was a policy beset by difficulties. The servants of the German state had to deal, however indirectly, with unpleasant facts of revolution, with the *demi-monde* of revolutionaries in exile, and also with the subtle distinctions among the various revolutionary groups. Minister Diego Bergen, the trusted official in Wilhelmstrasse, the central office of the Foreign Ministry, who, after the Great War, served both the Weimar Republic and Hitler's régime as Ambassador to the Holy See, dealt with this policy efficiently from the beginning of 1915 till the end of 1917. He was in constant touch with Helphand, but not entirely dependent on him; he could distinguish between the more and less effective types of revolutionaries and he took them for what they were: enemies of the Tsarist régime and advocates of the cessation of hostilities and peace.

The policy bore the mark of the highest security rating; its outline becomes clear from the documents printed in this volume. Its implementation, carried out by many agents, is obscure to a degree. Often the search in the archives of the Foreign Ministry is unrewarding: the words 'the matter was settled by word of mouth' appear too often. As few records as possible were made; it is surprising that so large a number of relevant documents were recorded and preserved. This is often due to the urgency of the matter in hand: the amount of documents for April and November of 1917 is higher than for any other period. The return of the political émigrés after the March revolution and the German reaction to the Bolshevik seizure of power were matters urgent to both parties involved. In more tranquil periods, the men involved could be summoned to Berlin for consultations. No record of these talks was preserved.

Some of the men who took part in the formulation of German war-time policy recorded their experiences. But the memoirs of Ludendorff, Kühlmann, Hoffmann, or Erzberger[1] do not enlighten the reader much as to the official attitude towards the revolution in Russia. They may have been unaware of the consistency of the policy as Bergen conducted it; they may

---

[1] E. Ludendorff, *Meine Kriegserinnerungen*, Berlin, 1919; R. Kühlmann, *Erinnerungen*, Heidelberg, 1948; K. F. Nowak, *Die Aufzeichnungen des General-Majors Max Hoffmann*, Berlin, 1928; M. Erzberger, *Erlebnisse im Weltkrieg*, Stuttgart und Berlin, 1920.

have regarded it as an incident which should remain hidden in the government archives, or they may have just forgotten. Kühlmann certainly knew about it but chose to be uninformative in his memoirs. Ludendorff, when referring to Lenin's journey across Germany, did so with 'bated breath'.

The committee of the Reichstag, inquiring, in the early years of the Weimar Republic into the causes of the downfall of the German Empire,[1] served us no better. Interested, as this committee was, in the problem of 'responsibility' for the breakdown of 1918, it may have regarded this feature of German policy in the Great War as outside the scope of its inquiry. Some Social Democrat members of the Committee may have had reasons not to proceed with it. Yet in 1921 Bernstein, the prominent Social Democrat, wrote two articles for the *Volksrecht* discussing this aspect of German war-time policy.[2]

The terms in which it was discussed during and immediately after the war did much to obscure its outline and detail. Germany was referred to as the 'father of the Russian revolution', the Bolshevik leaders as 'agents of Germany', and their actions were described as 'subservient to the Imperial government'. This perhaps was understandable in the heat of the European conflagration. Now, forty years later, they appear out of date—in fact, there is no justification for employing them.[3]

The aims of the Imperial Government and of the left wing of the Russian revolutionaries coincided to a high degree. The willingness of this government to grant favours may have, on occasions, exceeded the willingness of the revolutionaries to accept them.

There is no evidence among the documents of the Foreign Ministry that Lenin, a circumspect man, was in direct contact with any of the official German agenicies. How much he knew

---

[1] *Die Ursachen des deutschen Zusammenbruches im Jahre 1918.* Published by the Parliamentary Commission of Enquiry, Berlin.

[2] Vorwärts, Morgenausgabe, 14 January 1921: 'Ein dunkles Kapitel', Abendausgabe, 20 January 1921: 'Meisterstück und Meisterschuld'.

[3] The publication of the Sisson Documents (*The German-Bolshevik Conspiracy*, War Information Series, No. 20, Washington, 1918) did much to obscure both the German policy and its effect on the course of the revolution in Russia. Though in 1919 the German government described the publication as wholly fraudulent (*Die Entlarvung der 'Deutsch-Bolshevistischen Verschwörung'*, with an introduction by the Premier, Philipp Scheidemann, Berlin, 1919; see also G. F. Kennan's article in the *Journal of Modern History*, volume XXVIII, No. 2, June 1956). When Weismann, the State Commissar for Public Order referred, in 1921, to a publication of the same set of documents in Switzerland in 1919, he wrote: 'The documents in this pamphlet were partly forged' (Film reference: K281/K096202).

about the activities of the men around him is difficult to tell.
Hanecki, alias Fürstenberg, and Radek, both officially Austro-
Hungarian subjects, did, as well as Helphand, have some
contacts with the Germans.[1] But it cannot be said even about
Radek and Fürstenberg, who had more contacts with the
Germans than anyone else among the Bolsheviks, that the
interests of the Imperial German government lay close to their
hearts. A socialist revolution was their aim. To achieve and
further it they were prepared to use every means.

The aim of this collection of documents is to give a picture
of the policy of the Imperial German government towards the
revolution in Russia and also of some of the information available to this government on which the policy was based.

The documents printed here divide into four periods: January 1915 till March 1917, from the time of the first records of
Germany's interest in the revolution till its outbreak in March.
The second period runs from March 1917 till the Bolshevik
seizure of power. It includes the transport of the Russian
revolutionaries through Germany. Lenin's contingent was the
first of these transports; later, a number of them was organized
from Switzerland and Belgium. The criterion the German
government used for their approval was the attitude of the men
who were to be allowed transit through Germany to the question
of continuation of the war.

The third period covers November and December 1917,
starting with the German reactions to the Bolshevik seizure of
power, and ending at the time of the failure of Radek's and
Helphand's plan for a conference on neutral territory and the
opening of the peace negotiations at Brest-Litovsk. No documents
on these negotiations are printed here: it is a feature of German–
Russian relations which has been well covered both by publications of original sources and by secondary works. The documents
in the German Foreign Ministry Archives, covering the Brest-
Litovsk negotiations, have been filmed and are available at the
Public Records Office in London and the National Archives in
Washington.

The two letters from Ludendorff and from Mirbach (documents Nos. 134 and 136) are a suitable epitaph to the German
policy towards the revolution in Russia.

[1] See document No. 112 and A 23291 in Russland Nr. 61, volume 154. Deputy
Chief of Staff in Berlin to the Foreign Ministry, 30 May 1918. A report, signed by
Müller, on a conversation with Jakob Hanecki.

A NOTE ON TRANSLATION, FILMING, AND ARCHIVAL REFERENCES

THE editor has attempted to reproduce a faithful translation of the German originals. With one exception (see document No. 125 and footnote) the full text of the documents is printed here. Anything not to be found in the original text is isolated by square brackets. All the marginalia commenting on the contents of the document are given in notes following the document.

The editor allowed himself the following licenses: all routine administrative references and marginalia have been omitted. This includes references to other documents which introduce nothing new. The editor has attempted to trace references to other documents and the less known names which appear on the following pages: his failure to do so is not indicated by footnotes. He has also tried to provide editorial notes and footnotes which are purely explanatory and contain no comment or speculation.

Those readers interested in the German originals, or in the exploration of avenues which this publication opens, can consult the relevant films in the Public Records Office. Apart from the majority of the mission files, some of the Grosses Hauptquartier papers and the relevant *Nachlässe*, it is to be hoped that all the documents printed here have been filmed. The editor had the good fortune to work on the original documents: the private filming, done by the various university and other institutions, and intended to supplement the official project filming, is not indicated in any way on the originals. The documents filmed officially bear a stamp, the so-called serial and frame number. Because of the diversity of manner in which this material has been filmed, the editor decided not to include any filming references.

The original archival references, used here, are a sufficient guide for the location of every document not only in the archives, but also on the film. The so-called Aktenzeichen (for instance: WK 2 secr or Russland Nr. 61) and the number of the volume are the most important indications as to the location of a document. Then there are the journal numbers (numbers with the letters A or AS preceding them), which indicate the location of a document in the file. Because of the German archivists' use of the description '-zu-' (*Verfügung*, or action taken)

not every document has a separate journal number. There are
sometimes two or more documents bearing the same number,
or even more than one number: this indicates that the text of
the document has some connexion with another document or
documents: it is either a continuation or a reply. Only the first
journal number (in case of documents which bear more than
one) is printed here. Apart from the journal numbers, the numbers of the incoming and outgoing telegrams and reports are
given as a further aid for the location of a document in the file.

LIST OF DOCUMENTS

APPENDIXES

1

The Under State Secretary to the State Secretary
(At the time at General Headquarters)

TELEGRAM NO. 76

A 934   Berlin, 9 January 1915

The Imperial Ambassador in Constantinople has sent the following telegram under No. 70.

'The well-known Russian Socialist and publicist, Dr. Helphand, one of the main leaders of the last Russian Revolution, who was exiled from Russia and has, on several occasions, been expelled from Germany, has for some time been active here as a writer, concerning himself chiefly with questions of Turkish economics. Since the beginning of the war, Parvus's attitude has been definitely pro-German. He is helping Dr. Zimmer in his support of the Ukrainian movement and he also rendered useful services in the founding of Batsarias's newspaper in Bucharest. In a conversation with me, which he had requested through Zimmer, Parvus said that the Russian Democrats could only achieve their aim by the total destruction of Czarism and the division of Russia into smaller states. On the other hand, Germany would not be completely successful if it were not possible to kindle a major revolution in Russia. However, there would still be a danger to Germany from Russia, even after the war, if the Russian Empire were not divided into a number of separate parts. The interests of the German government were therefore identical with those of the Russian revolutionaries, who were already at work. However, there was as yet a lack of cohesion between the various factions. The Mensheviks had not yet joined forces with the Bolsheviks, who had already gone into action. He saw it as his task to create a unity and to organize the rising on a broad basis. To achieve this, a congress of the leaders would first of all be needed—possibly in Geneva. He was prepared to take the necessary first steps to this end, but would need considerable sums of money for the purpose. He therefore requested an opportunity of presenting his plans in Berlin. He confidently expected an Imperial Circular holding out to the [German] Social Democrats the prospect of an immediate

B 6706   B

improvement in primary schools and in average working hours, as a reward for their patriotic attitude, to have a considerable effect not only on German Socialists serving in the Army, but also on Russians sharing his own political opinions. Parvus has today travelled via Sofia and Bucharest to Vienna, where he will have discussions with Russian revolutionaries. Dr. Zimmer will arrive in Berlin at the same time as Parvus, and will be available to arrange meetings with him.

In Parvus's opinion, action must be taken quickly, so that the new Russian recruits will arrive at the front already contaminated. Wangenheim'

It would seem advisable for the Foreign Ministry to receive Parvus.[1]   ZIMMERMANN

---

[1] The State Secretary replied to this telegram on 10 January: 'Please receive Dr. Helphand in Berlin. Jagow.' On the same day, telegrams were dispatched from the Foreign Ministry to Vienna (No. 142), Constantinople (No. 66), and Bucharest (No. 37), requesting these missions and Dr. Zimmer to keep Helphand's connexion with the Batsarias affair secret. A 1110 in WK 11c secr, volume 3.

2

The State Secretary to the Foreign Ministry

TELEGRAM NO. 40

A 1451   General Headquarters, 13 January 1915, 12.20 a.m.
                            Received: 13 January, 1.43 a.m.

We intend to send Riezler[1] to meeting with Russian Revolutionary Parvus in Berlin with more detailed instructions. Please telegraph time of Parvus's arrival to me here. Parvus must not know that Riezler comes from General Headquarters.

JAGOW

---

[1] Kurt Riezler, born 1882. In May 1913 Riezler became a Permanent Assistant in the Foreign Ministry. In August 1914 he was detailed to attend the Kaiser at the General Headquarters. In January 1915 he was transferred to the Imperial Chancery. In September 1917 Riezler went to the Legation in Stockholm as a Counsellor to run the newly created Russian section there. In April 1918 he was recalled to Berlin, and in the same month he left to work with Count Mirbach, the Minister in Moscow. After Mirbach's assassination in July Riezler carried on the business of the Legation until his recall to Berlin at the end of August 1918.

3

Herr Fröhlich to Minister Bergen at the Foreign Ministry

A 10739   Berlin, 26 March 1915

Subject: Dr. Alexander Helphand-Parvus

The Deutsche Bank has sent me the transfer note for a further 500,000 marks, which I enclose herewith.

I should like to draw your attention to my letter of 20 March, in which I observed that Dr. Helphand requires a total of one million marks,[1] exclusive of losses incurred in exchange, and that any such losses incurred in Copenhagen, Bucharest, and Zürich, together with any other expenses, will thus have to be borne by us.

I would therefore ask you to make the necessary transfer to the Deutsche Bank, so that I may be able to pay Dr. Helphand this difference also.

Yours, &c.,
FRÖHLICH

---

[1] Helphand submitted his memorandum on the revolution in Russia to the Foreign Ministry sometime at the beginning of March (see Appendix I). On 6 March 1915 Zimmermann wrote to Drews, the Under State Secretary of the Ministry of Interior, asking him to free Helphand from any restrictions as to travel inside Germany, usually imposed on Russian subjects, and to provide Helphand with a police passport which he could use for travel in the neutral countries (A 8268 in WK 11c secr, volume 5). The day after, Zimmermann wrote to the State Secretary of the Imperial Treasury, asking him for 2 million marks for the support of Russian revolutionary propaganda (AS 919, WK 11c secr, volume 5). This request was approved on 11 March 1915 (WK 11c secr, volume 6).

4

The State Secretary of the Foreign Ministry to the State Secretary of the Treasury

AS 3530   Berlin, 6 July, 1915

Five million marks are required here for the promotion of revolutionary propaganda in Russia. As this sum cannot be covered out of the funds at our disposal, I would like to request Your Excellency to put it at my disposal by charging it to Article VI, Section II of the extraordinary budget. I should be extremely grateful to Your Excellency if you would inform me what action is taken.[1]

JAGOW

[1] The request was granted on 9 July. AS 3632 in WK 11c secr, volume 7.

5

The Minister in Copenhagen to the Under State Secretary

AS 4285   14 August 1915

Your Excellency,

Dr. Helphand, with whom I have recently had repeated and detailed conversation, yesterday told me that he had received a telegram from Arthur Cohn's Verlag für Sozialwissenschaften in Munich, informing him that only the first part of his essay had arrived. With the permission of the Foreign Ministry, I had sent three further instalments, but these have not yet arrived in Munich. Dr. Helphand is worried because he is afraid that the essay may appear too late and not, as he intends, by 1 September at the outside. Perhaps Your Excellency could make sure that the dispatch of the manuscripts is undertaken *at once*.

I have now got to know Helphand better, and I think that there can be no question that he is an extraordinarily important man whose unusual powers I feel we *must* employ for the duration of the war and should, if at all possible, continue to use later on—whether we personally agree with his convictions or not. He has a plan, conceived on a grand scale, of which he has already completed the first part, but, if the plan is not to be placed in jeopardy, he must be put into a position allowing him to publish the whole treatise not later than 1 September. His intention is to work on the German Social Democrats with this essay, for he has evidence that there is a strong current of opinion among them which already regards Russia as 'defeated and prostrate on the ground' and which, setting out from this false premise, would now like to be sentimentally indulgent towards Russia. His aim is energetically to counter this very dangerous trend. He has therefore, for technical and practical reasons, made certain concessions to the Socialists in his essay, of which he does not himself approve but which he thinks must win him the degree of influence over the broad sections encompassed by the party as a whole necessary to assure him sufficient authority at this critical moment, and to allow him later to step forward with an independent programme entirely his own.

Helphand told me that he was quite prepared to make alterations if he were given suitable hints to this effect, but that he wished to insist that the manuscript be sent to the publisher. Any corrections or alterations required could be made by the readers in Munich.

This request seems perfectly justified to me, and I feel it necessary that it should be granted if Helphand's plan is not to be impeded. As soon as he has drawn public attention to himself, and he does not doubt that he will succeed in doing this, he wants, in the middle of September, to publish a second essay, directed specially at Russia. Immediately after this he intends to proceed to the preparation of leaflets.

Helphand told me that he had been received by Your Excellency and that he had had the opportunity of presenting his plans in person. Dr. Zimmer, with whom I spoke on the occasion of his last visit to Copenhagen, was going to report verbally on his most recent discussion with Helphand, so Your Excellency is presumably well informed about these plans. As far as I can see from here, they have the approval of the Foreign Ministry and the General Staff, whereas objections seem to have been raised by the Ministry of the Interior and the Imperial Office of the Interior [Reichsamt des Innern]. I think that it is undesirable that one-sided, and therefore short-sighted, objections, from whatever quarter, should be considered *at this moment*.

Otherwise we shall never achieve the great aim which I have before my eyes. I have the hope that we shall not only emerge from this war as the external victors and the greatest power in the world, but also that, after the tremendous test that the German workers, indeed—to avoid invidious comparisons—'the common man' *in particular*, have now undergone, we may be able confidently to try to bring those elements to co-operate who, before the war, stood apart and seemed unreliable, and to group them around the throne.

It *might perhaps* be risky to want to use the powers ranged behind Helphand, but it would *certainly* be an admission of our own weakness if we were to refuse their services out of fear of not being able to *direct* them.

I have not yet abandoned this hope.

Those who do not understand the signs of our times will never understand which way we are heading or what is at stake at this moment.

Your Excellency, this moment is too grave for us to indulge in sentimentality, so let me close.

Yours, &c.,

BROCKDORFF-RANTZAU

6

The Minister in Bern to the Chancellor

REPORT NO. 794

A 28659   Bern, 30 September 1915

The Estonian Keskula[1] has succeeded in finding out the conditions on which the Russian revolutionaries would be prepared to conclude peace with us in the event of the revolution being successful. According to information from the well-known revolutionary Lenin, the programme contains the following points:

1. The establishment of a republic.
2. The confiscation of large land-holdings.
3. The eight-hour working day.
4. Full autonomy for all nationalities.
5. An offer of peace without any consideration for France, but on condition that Germany renounces all annexations and war-reparations.

On Point 5, Keskula has observed that this condition does not exclude the possibility of separating those national states from Russia which would serve as buffer states.

6. The Russian armies to leave Turkey immediately—in other words, a renunciation of claims to Constantinople and the Dardanelles.
7. Russian troops to move into India.

I leave open the question as to whether great importance should in fact be attached to this programme, especially as Lenin himself is supposed to be rather sceptical of the prospects of the revolution. He seems to be extremely apprehensive of the counter-campaign recently launched by the so-called Social Patriots. According to Keskula's sources, this counter-movement is headed by the Socialists Axelrod, Alexinsky, Deutsch, Dneveinski, Mark Kachel, Olgin, and Plekhanov. They are unleashing vigorous agitation, and are supposed to have large financial resources, which they appear to draw from the government, at their disposal. Their activities could be all the more dangerous to the revolution as they are themselves old revolutionaries, and are therefore perfectly familiar with the techniques of revolution. In Kesküla's opinion, it is therefore essential that we should spring to the help of the revolutionaries of Lenin's movement in Russia at once. He will report on this matter in person in Berlin. According to his informants, the present moment should be favourable for overthrowing the government. More and more reports of workers' unrest are being received, and the dismissal of the Duma is said to have aroused universal excitement. However, we should have to act quickly, before the Social Patriots gain the upper hand.

I have the honour to enclose two agitationary publications of the Social Patriots, which they are supposed to be distributing in enormous quantities.[2]

Even if, as I have said, the prospects of a revolution are uncertain and Lenin's programme is therefore of doubtful value, its exploitation could still do invaluable service in enemy territory. If skilfully distributed it could, in my opinion, be especially effective in France, in view of the notorious ignorance of the French in foreign, and particularly Russian affairs. If I receive no instructions from Your Excellency to the contrary, I shall give it to various French confidential agents for distribution among the ranks of the opposition. I can imagine that, by opening the prospect of a separate peace between Germany and the Russian Democrats, which would, of course, involve the loss of the French billions, one could provide the opposition with an extremely valuable trump card to play against M. Delclassé and in favour of a separate peace with us.[3]

Lenin's programme must not, of course, be made public, first because its publication would reveal our source, but also because its discussion in the press would rob it of all its value. I feel that it should be put out in an aura of great secrecy, so that it creates a belief that an agreement with powerful Russian circles is already in preparation.

Quite apart from the French aspect, I would ask you first of all to discuss this information with Kesküla, so that nothing may be spoiled by premature publication.
                                                              ROMBERG

[1] Kesküla was a member of the Estonian National Committee, working, in Switzerland and in Sweden, for the independence of his country from the Russian Empire. He was in contact with the German Legation in Bern from September 1914. Later, he worked with Steinwachs, the German agent (see document No. 12).

In April 1917 Kesküla apparently negotiated with the representatives of the Allied countries, especially of England and Russia, in Stockholm. When he got to know about these negotiations, Steinwachs dropped him. His activities are well documented in one of the Bern mission files, entitled 'Kesküla'. Cf. O. H. Gankin and H. H. Fisher, *The Bolsheviks and the World War*, Stanford University Press, 1940, p. 249.

² Only one of these enclosures remains in the file, the other was lost. It is a collection of essays entitled 'Voina'; Axelrod and Plekhanov were two of the contributors.

³ Jagow's marginal note: 'I regard a distribution in France as dangerous; nothing ever remains discreet there. If this became public our work in Russia would become much more difficult, and the measures against the revolutionaries would be tightened. I shall telegraph Romberg to this effect.' The telegram (No. 1081) was dispatched on 4 October (Russland Nr. 61, volume 123).

7

The Minister in Copenhagen to the Chancellor

REPORT NO. 489

AS 6213   21 December 1915

Dr. Helphand, who returned from Berlin yesterday, visited me today and gave me his report on the results of his journey. He emphasized that he had been extremely civilly received in all the most important government offices, and that he had been given the definite impression that his suggestions had found approval with authoritative circles, both in the Foreign Ministry and in the Treasury. With reference to his financial plan,[1] he had been given to understand that the State Secretary of the Treasury would have to decide whether there were any objections to his project from the point of view of the Imperial economy. In the course of a detailed discussion with State Secretary Helfferich he had been convinced that the State Secretary regarded his project very favourably, and that he not only agreed with it out of political considerations, but also recognized its utility from the less specific point of view of the Imperial economy.

The State Secretary of the Treasury had only expressed doubts as to the immediate technical practicability of the project, saying that a delay of eight to ten months would be required. At the same time, State Secretary Helfferich had pointed out that certain difficulties might be encountered in maintaining the absolute security which was essential for the technical preparations.

Dr. Helphand stressed that, in these circumstances, there was even more reason to take the preparations in hand at once, since we shall in any case have to reckon with a third winter campaign and the course of action which he advocates may therefore become imperative.

Dr. Helphand continued by saying that about 20 million roubles would be required to get the Russian revolution completely organized. This total could not possibly be distributed at once, as there would then be a danger of its source being discovered. However, in view of the fact that the beginning of the action was imminent, he had suggested at the Foreign Ministry that the sum of one million roubles should at once be put at the disposal of his confidential agent. This confidential agent entirely shared his view that the revolution would be set in motion about 9–22 January and that, even if it did not immediately take hold of the whole country, it would certainly prevent any return to stable conditions from taking place. In 1905 the bourgeois parties had supported the revolution and had voluntarily paid the wages of the striking workers. Now, however, the bourgeoisie was unfavourable to the movement and the revolutionary committee was therefore forced to bear the entire cost. On his return in about a week, his confidential agent would immediately start on the organization of connexions between the various revolutionary centres, but this could not be done without considerable financial means.

In the circumstances, Dr. Helphand asked me to reiterate the request, which he had made personally in Berlin, for the sum he had named to be put at the disposal of his confidential agent. He expressly stated that speed was essential, as his confidential agent could not delay his return to Petrograd any longer but would definitely travel to Russia in a week at the most, even if he had not received the requested sum within that time.

I should like to request Your Excellency to send me instructions by telegram so that I can inform Dr. Helphand. May I also say that his suggestion is not, in my humble opinion, any attempt to press his own interests, but springs from practical considerations with no secondary personal aims.

BROCKDORFF-RANTZAU

---

[1] Helphand maintained that confidence in the rouble could be shattered in Russia and abroad by certain measures of the German Treasury. See report No. 463, the Minister in Copenhagen to the Chancellor, 30 November 1915; in WK 110 secr, volume 10.

8

The State Secretary of the Treasury to the Under State Secretary

AS 6235   Berlin, 26 December 1915

Dear Zimmermann,

I herewith return Count Brockdorff-Rantzau's report with many thanks.[1]

I did in fact treat Helphand with rather more restraint than he described at Copenhagen. In my opinion, there is a great deal of fantasy in his plans, particularly in his so-called 'financial plan', in which I hardly think we shall be able to involve ourselves. On the other hand, it would be worth discussing the possibility of putting at his disposal the million roubles for which he asks for the purposes of his propaganda. If the Foreign Ministry considers this expense both useful and justified, I shall not oppose it. In that case I would ask you to forward an application in the usual way, referring in it to our personal agreement.

With hearty, if somewhat belated Christmas greetings.

Yours, &c.,

HELFFERICH

[1] Document No. 7.

9

The State Secretary to the Minister in Copenhagen

TELEGRAM NO. 952

AS 6213   Berlin, 26 December 1915

In reply to report No. 489

Your Excellency is authorized to pay one million roubles to Helphand. The corresponding sum should be drawn from the Legation Cashier [Legationskasse].   JAGOW

Note for Count Pourtales.

Count Rantzau will have to be informed that Dr. Helfferich's opinion of H[elphand]'s fantastic financial project is by no means as favourable as H[elphand] thinks.   JAGOW

10

Herr Steinwachs to Minister Bergen

AS 185   Berlin, 18 January 1916

I have the honour to send Your Excellency the following:[1]

1. A letter from Kesküla, dated 9 January 1916.
2. A translation of the brochure of the central committee of the Russian Social Democratic Workers' Party.
3. A translation of the publication on the execution of the Russian volunteers in France.

STEINWACHS

Enclosure:

Stockholm, 9 January 1916

Dear Director,[2]

I was told today that something had arrived for me. I shall be going to the Mission tomorrow and will use the opportunity to deliver this letter. It is already 10.30 p.m. and I must be brief, especially as I have today been negotiating from 10 a.m. until 10.15 p.m.

The clearing up of the Russian situation here, as far as organization is concerned, has been completed today and, at the same time, the clearing up of the confused situation in Russia has begun. I have great hopes of the action which has been set in motion. In my last letter I already indicated the nature of the results it is hoped to achieve, when I wrote: 'The situation demands an extension of my activities, and this extension must therefore take place.'

I now have an ideal new collaborator and, through him, the possibility of working on the whole of Scandinavia as well as the whole of Russia. A small private publishing concern is to be set up to bring out pamphlets about Russia, and an information sheet, printed in Swedish, is to be founded for the revolutionary movement. In addition, Denmark and Norway, and possibly other European countries, are to be kept regularly informed of developments within the Russian revolutionary movement. For the distribution of our literature we have at our disposal the existing highly developed apparatus of the Socialist youth organizations here (over 600 hawkers in Sweden alone).

At the same time, a central office for the support of the revolutionary movement (through agitation and collections of money) is to be set up, and will be open to the public. This central office will support the Russian movement—both morally and materially—quite openly and without consulting the leaders or Russian revolutionary centres outside Russia. For the latter group it will simply supply the means for publishing literature to be sent to Russia and, possibly, for its actual transport. At the end of this week, my confidential agent will be travelling to Russia (for about four weeks) to discuss financial support from Western Europe with the revolutionary centres inside Russia. At the same time he will settle where and how information about the Russian movement is to be sent to him. The agent in question has first-class connexions, so that the discussions will, I hope, go smoothly. The position here had to be put back on a healthy footing because considerable corruption had crept in. (Embezzlement at the expense of the revolutionary movement, presentation of false facts in order to extract money, &c.) I therefore threw the offenders overboard, cleared up the situation and increased both the scale and the intensity of the undertaking. This has made such demands on me, that I have had no time for anything else.

Tomorrow I shall begin my survey of the Russian situation and, if nothing else of particular importance arises, I shall also deal with the *Frankfurter Zeitung*.

Tomorrow I shall be sending you a telegram saying that the mail from Stockholm to Switzerland is being searched for Russian documents. Today, or in the next few days, some highly interesting revolutionary documents from Russia are being sent to Lenin. I read through them yesterday, but had no chance to make copies of them. Could you please be so kind as to return them to me, as it is essential that some of them be copied and distributed in Russia. They call for an armed rising and for the organization of military mutinies. One of them— the product of a Moscow 'Welfare Committee'—which suggests a dictatorial Directorate for Russia, to consist, among other people, of MM. Guchkov, Lvov and Kerenski (*sic!*), is extremely amusing. Judging by its comico-sentimental torrent of verbiage, this must be a call from the right wing of the so-called 'Popular Nationalists' [*Volkstuemler*]. Some of these documents are extremely interesting for the insight which they give into the stage of development reached by the revolutionary movement at the end of 1915. They already show all the symptoms which appeared in the summer of 1905. On the ideological side, the present Russian revolutionary movement must be regarded, in its essentials, as being perfectly mature and ready. All that can possibly remain to be done is some further formulation of details. The transformation of the revolutionary movement into an active one is now only a question of agitation and, above all, of organization. I should particularly like to recommend these documents to the attention of Baron von L.[3] Due to their extremely poor printing and preparation, the leaflets have only cultural and historical value, but they will perhaps remind you of your promise to send some typographical material. I would ask you to handle the papers with all possible care, as I do not want Lenin's joy at the receipt of his Russian Christmas present decreased in any way. In other words, they should first be sent here. From here they will be returned for forwarding to the addressee. At the end of the week, the second Russian brochure of the Central Committee of the Russian Social Democrats (i.e. Lenin) will be appearing. It lay in the pending tray for two months (while I was in Berlin) because the money which I had paid out before my departure had been stolen with typical Russian sang-froid. Yesterday I paid the sum out again. I have already indicated what reprisals I took. If this sort of thing happens in and around the Central Committee, I dare not think what must be happening on the fringes. Even the revolution has to be forced on these Russians with police truncheons in order to prevent them from making off with it. I mention this as an illustration of all the complications that have to be faced here. I will write more later.[4]

Yours, &c.
A. Stein[5]

[1] Only the first enclosure, i.e. the letter from Keskula to Steinwachs, is printed here. The German translation of the two pamphlets can be found in the same file, WK 11c secr, volume 11.

[2] i.e. Steinwachs, who was an agent of the General Staff. Apart from his political work in the field of separatist and revolutionary movements in Russia he had some industrial interests in Sweden. He was working independently of Helphand, but had contacts with him from the summer of 1915. In a request to the Admiralty to print Russian revolutionary propaganda, Zimmermann wrote in June 1915: 'Steinwachs is responsible for the composition of the propaganda literature' (A 17293 in WK 11c secr, volume 7). In the summer of 1916 Steinwachs was sent on a special mission to Rumania. After his return in the winter of 1916 he was sent back to Stockholm and attached, with his assistants, to the German Legation there.

In the spring of 1918 the Swedish and Danish police became interested in the activities of German agents on their territory. Rondorf, one of Steinwachs's accomplices, was deported, Helphand's flats in Stockholm and Copenhagen were searched, and in May 1918 Hülsen, the head of the Political Section of the Deputy General Staff, recalled Steinwachs and his assistants (Count Adelmann, Buchholtz, Appenroth, and Stroh) from Stockholm. In the last stages of the war Steinwachs conducted anti-Swedish propaganda from Finland.

[3] This was probably Baron Langwerth von Simmern in the Foreign Ministry.

[4] On 1 February Kesküla dispatched another long letter to Steinwachs (Bern mission, file 'Kesküla'). He complained of complications which followed Helphand's attempt to see Bukharin at the end of January 1915. Bukharin apparently refused to see Helphand. At the same time, the excitable Russian *emigrés* started to suspect Kesküla. But, by the time he wrote the letter, all damage, according to Kesküla, had been repaired. He wrote: 'How helpless these Russians are as far as purposeful organization is concerned is proved by the fact that Bukharin was denouncing me, seeking information about me; during the day he was running round the town looking for my address, and at night he could not sleep. At the same time, the enclosed pamphlet was printed at my expense, without Bukharin knowing this, and yet to his great pleasure.'

The enclosed pamphlet by Bukharin was entitled *The War and the Working Class.* In Kesküla's opinion it was suitable for distribution among the broad masses and he recommended Steinwachs that a larger edition should be printed on rice paper. The edition on normal paper was intended for distribution among the revolutionaries abroad; a large part of the first rice-paper edition had, according to Kesküla, reached the other side of the Finnish frontier safely.

Kesküla also reported that his agent, who had first-class connexions and recommendations, had reached Petrograd. He commented that the amusing thing was that his agent also had a letter of introduction from Bukharin to Mme Bukharin.

In his letter, Kesküla divided his work into three phases: (1) work among the *emigrés* in Switzerland, (2) work in Stockholm, the Russian 'bridgehead', (3) direct connexion with Russia. Kesküla wrote that, with the departure of his agent for Petrograd, the third stage of his work had been reached.

[5] Kesküla's cover name.

11

The Minister in Copenhagen to the Chancellor

REPORT NO. 19

AS 293   23 January 1916

Dr. Helphand, who has returned to Copenhagen after spending three weeks in Stockholm, where he conferred with Russian revolutionaries, has told me the following, in confidence:

The sum of a million roubles which was put at his disposal, was immediately sent on, and has already reached Petrograd and been devoted to the purposes for which it was intended. Helphand insisted on beginning the action on 22 January. However, his confidential agents advised him against this with the utmost firmness, saying that immediate action would be premature, and painted the following picture of the present situation:

The decision of the organizations to launch into revolutionary action is still firm and unchanged, but, in the last two months, the political situation has altered in such a way that it now appears inadvisable to strike immediately.

The opposition of the bourgeois parties to a revolutionary rising has stiffened and is now, if anything, more determined than before. The government, too, has not been idle, and has certainly moved skilfully in an effort to counter the revolutionary movement. It has called several men who, before the war, were spokesmen of the revolutionaries to leading positions and has, in this way, considerably weakened the movement. Furthermore, it has taken measures to relieve the food shortage in Petrograd, which was threatening to become acute. Among other things, the passenger traffic between Petrograd and Moscow was stopped for a time to allow the rapid transport of food to Petrograd.

The most serious obstruction, however, is the attitude of the right wing, which would like to use a rising for its own purposes. In the revolutionary camp it is feared that, should there be a rising at this moment, the reactionaries would mingle with the ranks of the revolutionaries in order to give the movement the character of anarchy. The revolutionaries are not certain that they control the masses sufficiently to remain masters of the movement, should these masses get onto the streets. These are the considerations which are determining the postponement of the revolutionary rising until the moment when this certainty is realized.

The peace propaganda of the reactionaries is also compromising a rising which is intended to serve a revolutionary purpose. While all these factors are not regarded as strong enough to prevent a revolutionary rising, they are considered to be sufficiently important to make any premature rising inadvisable. It is not impossible that the summoning of the Duma may call forth further political conflicts and cause the revolutionary action to break out sooner than might be deduced from the present views of the leaders. The leaders of the revolutionary movement now hold the view that, in the circumstances and if no unexpected change develops in the situation, it is essential to continue to adopt a waiting position, in order to be sure, not only of bringing sufficient masses onto the streets, but also of being able to maintain control of them at the moment the signal is given.

The parties on the right are inclined towards making peace, and it is also thought that the government could be brought to favour peace. The attitude of the Minister of the Interior, Chvostov, is uncertain. While he stands in the closest possible connexion with the reactionary parties, he has, in a confidential conversation with leading personalities, said that he was 'the fore-most revolutionary of Russia' and that it was essential that Czar Nicholas be deposed. Chvostov arranged to be asked, at a session of a committee of the Duma, whether he was aware that there was a faction working for peace forming in Court circles. He answered that this was a false rumour and that he had expelled the person to whom it might refer, Mlle Vasilchikov, from Petrograd.

According to an extremely reliable source, the whole of the Entente Treaty was read out at the congress of the right-wing parties. On this occasion, particular attention was drawn to a clause stating that, in the event of the royal palaces being threatened by an enemy or of a revolution breaking out in the country, Russia would be free to conclude a separate peace. There is no doubt that this document was read out, but it remains questionable whether or not it was authentic.

BROCKDORFF-RANTZAU

1 2

Herr Steinwachs to Minister Bergen

MEMORANDUM

AS 1631   Berlin, 8 May 1916

According to a statement of account dated 28 April, the credit of 130,000 marks, paid to me by the Foreign Ministry at the end of September 1915 for Russian propaganda, is not only totally exhausted, but closed with a deficit of 1,011.93 marks. This deficit was paid to me today by the Mission Cashier.

Your Excellency later, i.e. in December 1915, agreed to the payment of a further 60,000 marks, which Herr Kesküla was to spend in three monthly instalments on Russian propaganda. Of this sum I succeeded in retaining 50,000 marks, through savings on the credit of 130,000 marks. I have since supplied most of the remaining 10,000 marks out of my own means. Furthermore, the original credit has been used to support several more or less successful new undertakings and preparations, about which I have received verbal reports from time to time.

Finally, as agreed with your Excellency, 2,000 roubles and 1,500 Swiss francs were put at the disposal of the Political Section of the General Staff of the Army for Prince Matchabelli's undertaking.[1]

Considerable sums will be needed at once, or in the next few weeks or months, for the following undertakings:

1. In the last few months, Kesküla has opened up numerous new connexions with Russia, and he has on several occasions sent Scandinavian Socialists to Russia with introductions to leading personalities who so effectively enlightened them on the subject of the situation in Russia, that the reports published later aroused admiration amongst the various Socialist circles in the North. He has also maintained his extremely useful contact with Lenin, and has transmitted to us the contents of the situation reports sent to Lenin by Lenin's confidential agents in Russia. Kesküla must therefore continue to be provided with the necessary means in the future. Taking into account the exceptionally unfavourable exchange conditions, 20,000 marks per month should be just sufficient.

2. Litchev has now begun all his preparations (i.e. the offices in Stockholm and Haparanda) and has started to gather together all the Russian revolutionaries living in the various cities of Scandinavia in order to exploit their particular capabilities. He has had several very effective pamphlets printed in Stockholm, and has got them into Russia by a safe route. I therefore humbly request your permission to pay him 6,000 marks per month for the next three months.

3. Klein has also successfully introduced a number of important information sheets and small pamphlets into Russia. He has also set up an information service on the station at Stockholm, which explains to Russians returning from America and Canada the possibilities of avoiding mobilization in the Russian army, or, if their mobilization is unavoidable, convinces them, with pictures and by word of mouth, of the good treatment enjoyed by Russian prisoners of war in Germany. A simple picture-book, containing pictures of prisoner-of-war camps in Germany and of the life led by the prisoners in them, together with notes detailing the conditions there, is to be produced for this information service and also for distribution in the Russian trenches. Klein receives a salary of 300 marks per month, and the expenses incurred by his other activities will now amount to 700 marks per month. I would also ask you to put 3,000 to 4,000 marks at my disposal for the printing costs of the proposed picture-book.

4. I estimate the cost of our private printing establishment,

which is to start work this month, at 800 to 1,000 marks per month, for the moment. This printing works will then do all the necessary printing for Klein, Litchev and Kesküla.

5. The various costs for translation and printing of a book describing conditions in Russia by means of reports by Russian members of the Duma, which is to be printed in several languages, will probably amount to 10,000 marks.

I therefore request Your Excellency to agree and provide the following sums:[2]

		M
1.	Kesküla. Remainder of March, April, May, June	70,000
2.	Litchev. May, June, July	18,000
3.	Klein. April, May, June (Salary, Organization, Book)	7,000
4.	Printing works in Stockholm	2,000
5.	Duma reports	10,000
6.	Smaller undertakings, travel, small printing jobs, &c.	23,000
		M130,000

May I ask Your Excellency to transfer this sum to Deposit Account A in the Deutsche Bank?   STEINWACHS

[1] The Georgian separatist movement.
[2] Marginal note by Bergen for Mathieu, in the Personnel Department of the Foreign Ministry: 'Presented with the request to transfer the sum of 130,000 marks. Will you please see to it that this sum is transferred from the Russian account?'

13

The Minister in Bern to the Chancellor

REPORT NO. 1885

AS 3061   24 August 1916

Subject: Connexions with a Russian Social Revolutionary

Baron Hennet, who has been attached to the Military Office of the Austro-Hungarian Legation, yesterday, with the approval of the Austro-Hungarian Military Attaché, introduced me to a Russian Social Revolutionary called Zivin. The immediate reason for this was that Zivin wishes to travel from here to Sweden through Germany.

Baron Hennet told me the following about Zivin:

Over a year ago, quite by chance, Zivin got to know the

Austro-Hungarian Consul at Davos, who introduced him to the
Austro-Hungarian Legation. Zivin belongs to the Social
Revolutionary party and has excellent connexions with its leading members, e.g. Chernov and Bobrov. He took part in the
revolutionary movement of 1905 and 1906, was in prison for a
while, but was soon released and, since then, has lived in
Switzerland. He promised to set revolutionary and pacifist
propaganda in motion among the Russian prisoners of war in
Austria, and in Russia itself.

After this, Zivin was twice sent to Austria, once in the autumn
of last year and once at the beginning of this year. Baron Hennet
stressed that the relevant military authorities had formed an
excellent impression of Zivin and had declared themselves
ready to put considerable financial means at his disposal.

At the time, Zivin visited several prisoner-of-war camps. It
was also intended that he should have an opportunity of finding
a few suitable people, who were later to be sent to Russia from
Switzerland.

Later, Zivin for a time provided the Russian prisoners in
Austria with suitable literature from Switzerland. However, the
sending of publications and books met with difficulties because
some of the Austrian camp commandants refused to distribute
Socialist literature among their prisoners.

Zivin subsequently had to abandon his plan to send freed
prisoners to Russia, as he did not have enough time, during his
short visits to the prisoner-of-war camps, to test the reliability
of the prisoners who were presented to him. In these circumstances he did not want to risk the possibility of the prisoners
betraying him and his plans after their arrival in Switzerland.

However, he did send a number of other people to Russia,
and these have worked for his party there. Amongst other things,
printing works have been set up where manifestos have been
printed, and these have been widely distributed, especially
through the military organization founded by the Social
Revolutionaries.

Zivin showed Baron Hennet a few of these manifestos, some
of them in their original form. He has also reported regularly
to Baron Hennet on the activities of the Social Revolutionary
party and of the committees which it has in many places, and
on conditions inside Russia. He was not able to give detailed
proofs of the success of his confidential agents, but, in view of
the exceptional difficulty of maintaining communications with
Russia, this is not really surprising. However, Zivin claims that

certain terrorist acts which he had predicted and which then
actually took place, were the outcome of the activities of men
of his party. Zivin had also been in an awkward position because
his party could not be allowed to know the source of the money
which had been put at his disposal. He had, in any case, been
very modest in his demands; in the eleven months during which
he has been connected with the Austro-Hungarian Legation he
has only received a total of 140,000 francs.

Baron Hennet told me that both he and Colonel von Einem
[the Military Attaché] were very satisfied with Zivin's work,
and that they had confidently expected more useful services from
him in the future.

About three weeks ago, however, the Austro-Hungarian High
Command suddenly declared that Zivin had 'shown insufficient
energy' and that no further payments should therefore be made
to him.

Zivin was thus put into a very awkward position. In expecta-
tion of further financial support, he had entered into obligations
which he cannot now honour. He is therefore forced to instruct
his confidential agents to cease their activities, or at least to
limit them severely. He now wants to travel through Germany
to Sweden in order to explore the possibility of finding funds
there for the continuation of his activities. However, he would
prefer to stay in Switzerland, as he can work better and more
safely here. One of the most important members of his party,
Bobrov, who is in continual contact with Russia, is living here,
and Zivin seems to attach great value to his connexions with
him. The leader of the party, Chernov, was also here until last
May, but he left for Russia at that time, and, since then, Zivin
has heard nothing from him.

Baron Hennet confessed to me that he was extremely sorry
not to be able to go on supporting Zivin, whom he regarded as
an honest man. Even the High Command had emphasized that
they did not distrust Zivin: they were merely of the opinion that
he lacked energy. It is not clear what it actually was that induced
the Austrian High Command to drop Zivin. It would appear
that they had illusions about the possibility of speedily creating
a revolutionary mood in Russia, and that they had even expected immediately apparent military effects on the organization behind the front. When Brusilov's offensive disappointed
these expectations, then the Austro-Hungarian army may have
lost patience and decided that further expense towards these
ends was superfluous.

Zivin, who made a not unfavourable impression on me, rightly stresses the fact that no revolutionary organization worthy of the name existed before the war, and that all this had to be created during the war in face of enormous difficulties. The most important consideration was that the wealthy Liberal circles who, at the time of the revolutionary movement of 1905, had supported the efforts of the Social Revolutionaries, had become patriots at the outbreak of the World War and had come out in favour of war. In these circumstances, the revolutionary movement could only make slow progress and was dependent on outside support. Nevertheless, the organization was gaining more and more ground, both behind the front and at the front itself. Its followers numbered hundreds of thousands, and even many army officers were members of the party. More and more people were now growing weary of the war. The next aim of the Social Revolutionary party was to work for a quick end to the war. The party's real programme could not be put into effect until the war had ended. On this aim to end the war quickly, the interests of the party and of the Central Powers therefore ran parallel to one another. The furtherance of revolutionary propaganda would, on the one hand, make it more difficult for the Russian government to continue the war, and, on the other hand, would also strengthen the desire of the reactionary government for peace.

Zivin gave me some information about the progress of the revolutionary propaganda, and this agreed on many points with the information I have received from the other side, e.g. from Kesküla.

Zivin would be extremely sorry now suddenly to have to give up his support of his friends. The whole organization had been well run-in, and it would be a great pity if it now had to be largely broken up. His friends in the party could hardly expect to be granted the necessary funds from another source at the present time. He would nevertheless be quite prepared to try and find these funds in Stockholm, and he would therefore be grateful for permission to travel through Germany, as he could not count on reaching Sweden via England, since the English were, at the moment, only allowing Russians to travel to Sweden in very rare and exceptional cases. Of course there was a danger that his journey through Germany might compromise him with his party friends, and they must naturally not be allowed to know that he was in contact with us and the Austrians.

When I asked him how much money he needed to continue

his work, he answered that he required 25,000 francs, which would last for the first three or four weeks. However, he would have to receive this sum very soon, as he had already kept his friends waiting for three weeks through no fault of his own, and would have to give them a definite answer in the immediate future as to whether they could continue to count on his support or not.

I naturally limited myself to hearing what M. Zivin had to say, without giving him any kind of promise. I do not know whether we have connexions with the Russian Socialists, and I am therefore not in a position to judge whether a connexion with M. Zivin would be desirable for us. However, judging by what Baron Hennet told me about Zivin, there seems to me to be some reason to believe that we could establish extremely useful contacts with the Social Revolutionaries through him. In my opinion, there is no doubt that we could derive advantages from such contacts. It is, of course, hard to prophecy how far, apart from the information from Russia which we could receive through Zivin, we could count on practical action on the part of his confidential agents. Baron Hennet thinks that there is no reason to doubt the truth of Zivin's assurance that we could count on the Social Revolutionary party to succeed in helping to shorten the war considerably. Zivin himself says—and, in my opinion, this speaks in his favour—that he cannot yet say definitely what measure of success his friends would have or when they could act decisively. This would depend on the overall situation. However, they were certain to be successful in the long run.

Since I am not sufficiently well informed about the situation in Russia, I must beg to leave the decision as to whether or not I should open relations with M. Zivin to Your Excellency. I would recommend that contact be maintained on a probationary basis in any case, and that Zivin's successes be observed for a few weeks. The advantage of a connexion with Zivin lies in the fact that he is himself an active member of a Russian party who is not suspected of having relations with us, whereas those agents whose relations with us are known do not enjoy any credit in their party, and can therefore neither find out much, nor exercise any influence on developments in any sphere. It would certainly be a pity if the whole apparatus which has been built up with Austrian funds were to be wasted and not used, quite apart from the fact that the propaganda, which is indubitably serving our aims, would considerably diminish if the subsidies stopped.

I would therefore suggest that M. Zivin be given the 25,000 francs he needs, but that he be told that we must reserve our final decision as to whether we intend to maintain a permanent connexion with him.[1]

Since M. Zivin must inform his agents immediately whether or not they are to cease work, I would ask for a reply as soon as possible.

I should also like to ask Your Excellency to treat this matter with the utmost confidence, as Baron Hennet gave me the information in strictest confidence. The matter was discussed only between the Austro-Hungarian Legation and the Austro-Hungarian High Command: Austro-Hungarian diplomatic circles have no knowledge of it. It might also be advisable not to make any inquiries from the Austro-Hungarian High Command, even though Baron Hennet assured me that he had no objections to such inquiries being made. I nevertheless think that an inquiry might make some unpleasantness for Baron Hennet and Colonel von Einem.

ROMBERG

[1] On 30 August the State Secretary approved the request for 25,000 francs, but reserved his right to make a decision on further relations with Zivin (Telegram No. 599 in WK 11c secr, volume 15). Before January 1917, when Zivin went to Norway via Germany, he received three more payments of 25,000 francs each. On 19 February he returned to Bern. His request for a further 30,000 francs was turned down by the Secretary of State on 6 March (Telegram No. 271). On 17 March Zimmermann changed his mind and approved the payment, and promised three further instalments of 5,000 francs each. Documents on Zivin's connexions with the Minister in Bern are in the subsequent volumes of WK 11c secr. Cf. document No. 56 and footnote 1.

Editorial note

Between September 1916 and March 1917 the Foreign Ministry continued to receive regular reports on the situation in Russia, and to support various separatist movements, especially the Finnish and the Ukrainian. But the only evidence of the continued interest of the Foreign Ministry in the revolution in Russia is the reports from Romberg on his contacts with Zivin, the Social Revolutionary.

Whatever the hopes of the Imperial government may have been for the conclusion of a separate peace with the existing order in Russia in the summer and autumn of 1916, the Germans themselves signed their death warrant by issuing the Imperial Manifesto on 6 November, concerning the future of the occupied territory in Poland. No Russian government, apart from a revolutionary one, could have been expected to sign a peace treaty with an enemy who planned to detach a large part of territory on Russia's western frontier.

At the same time, in November 1916, Zimmermann took over the direction of German foreign policy from Jagow. He remained in office, assisted by two Under State Secretaries, Bussche and Stumm, till Kühlmann replaced him in August 1917. The first intimation of the March revolution reached Wilhelmstrasse on 23 February. Lucius reported from Stockholm: 'I hear from an important Entente personality who has just arrived here from Petrograd that a mighty internal political change is being prepared there. Events of the most far-reaching importance can be expected within this month' (AS 791 in WK 11c secr, volume 19).

On 1 April 1917 the Foreign Ministry sent a request to the Treasury for a further 5 million marks to be used for political purposes in Russia. The request was approved on 3 April (AS 1091 and AS 1295 in WK 11c secr, volume 19). Because of the large amounts allocated, Count Roedern, the new State Secretary of the Treasury, asked the Foreign Ministry for what purposes these funds had been employed. Once again, because of the confidential nature of the request, the matter was settled by word of mouth between the two Ministries.

From the spring of 1915 till the autumn of 1916 the policy of support of the revolution in Russia was, to a high degree, a matter of administrative routine for the Foreign Ministry. At the same time, attempts at a separate peace between the established régime in Russia and Germany were carried on by conservative politicians, bankers, industrialists, and members of noble houses on both sides. After the first Russian revolution the picture changed profoundly.

After March, the Germans were faced with a revolutionary government; they had to distinguish between those revolutionaries willing to conclude a separate peace and those inclined to continue the struggle against the Central Powers on the side of the Entente. The Warburgs and Kolyshkos, the Stinneses and Bebutovs disappeared from the limelight.

Their place was taken by Social Democrat politicians and a few members of other parties of the majority in the Reichstag. The Social Democrats, remembering the inheritance of the Second International, and seeing that the Tsarist régime, to them the 'bulwark of European reaction', had disappeared, made repeated and uncoordinated attempts to come to an agreement with the Russian revolutionaries, often over the head of their own government. They were zealous to reap the glory of bringing about, if not a general, at least a separate peace. The German government, still pursuing its policy of a separate peace in order to reduce the war to a one-front engagement, had often to intervene and put a stop to such meritorious, but unofficial activities.

14

The Minister in Copenhagen to the Foreign Ministry

TELEGRAM NO. 476

A 9384   21 March 1917, 12.55 p.m.
                              Received: 21 March, 4.00 p.m.

Dr. Helphand, with whom I discussed events in Russia, explained that, in his opinion, the conflict was now primarily between the moderate liberals and the Socialist wing. He had no doubt that the latter would gain the upper hand. However, the victory of the Social Democrats in Russia would mean peace. The men at present in power apparently wished to continue the war, and the leaders of the faction in favour of this policy were Miliukov and Guchkov. Both these men would try to delay the convening of the Constituent National Assembly, since they knew that the moment the National Assembly had any influence, the continuation of the war would be out of the question.

When I asked him what he considered the attitude of the army to be, Dr. Helphand replied that there might well be some desire to continue the war among the Officer Corps, and especially among the higher-ranking officers, but that the rank and file wanted peace, and that it was highly significant that the ordinary soldiers, without exception, fraternized with the workers.

Dr. Helphand believes that as soon as the amnesty for political offenders comes into force, there will be an opportunity to work effectively against Miliukov and Guchkov through direct contact with the Socialists.

BROCKDORFF-RANTZAU

15

The State Secretary to the Foreign Ministry Liaison Officer at General Headquarters

TELEGRAM NO. 461

AS 1125   Berlin, 23 March 1917

The Imperial Minister in Bern has sent the following telegram:
'Federal Counsellor [Bundesrat] Hoffmann has been told that

leading Russian revolutionaries here wish to return to Russia via Germany as they are afraid to travel via France because of the danger from submarines. Please send instructions in case applications to this effect should be made to me. Romberg.'

Since it is in our interests that the influence of the radical wing of the Russian revolutionaries should prevail, it would seem to me advisable to allow transit to the revolutionaries there. I would therefore support the granting of permission. Would Your Excellency please inform the High Command of the Army and ask for their opinion in this matter?

ZIMMERMANN

16

The Liaison Officer at General Headquarters to the Foreign Ministry

TELEGRAM NO. 371

AS 1148   25 March 1917, 12.15 a.m.
                                   Received: 25 March, 1.15 a.m.

In reply to telegram No. 461.

High Command of the Army instructs me to telegraph as follows: 'No objections to transit of Russian revolutionaries if effected in special train with reliable escort. Organization can be worked out between representatives of IIIb[1] in Berlin and Foreign Ministry.'

LERSNER

[1] The military Passport Office.

17

The Under State Secretary to the Minister in Bern

TELEGRAM NO. 348

AS 1148   Berlin, 26 March 1917

Special train will be under military escort. Hand-over at frontier-station, either Gottmadingen or Lindau, by responsible official of the consulate. Send information immediately concerning date of journey and list of names. Information must reach here four days before frontier-crossing. General Staff unlikely to object to individual personalities. In any case, return transport to Switzerland is guaranteed.   BUSSCHE

18

The Minister in Bern to the Chancellor

REPORT NO. 879

A 10630   29 March 1917

The Imperial Consul-General in Basle received the following information from a reliable source: 'The Russian socialist and nihilist committees in Switzerland, in Bern, Zürich, and Geneva, have asked the representatives of the German press in Switzerland to work in their newspapers against Germany's undertaking an offensive against Russia, because this would disturb the peace plans of these committees.'[1]
                                                    ROMBERG

[1] The German government received a similar request from Ferdinand, King of Bulgaria. Ferdinand advised Oberndorff, the German Minister in Sofia, that it would be a mistake to exploit Russia's weakness and launch an offensive against her. (The Minister in Sofia to the Foreign Ministry, 24 March 1917. AS 1168 and AS 1169 in WK 2 secr, volume 31. All the documents referred to in this note are in the same file.)

A German offensive, it was argued at the time, would strengthen English influence in Russia and would contribute to the political unification of the hitherto divided nation. (The Liaison Officer at General Headquarters to the Foreign Ministry, 26 March 1917, AS 1173.) On 27 March the State Secretary replied to the telegrams from Sofia that no attack was being planned on the Russian front. Cf. *Die Aufzeichnungen des Generalmajors Max Hoffmann*, Berlin, 1930, volume 2, pp. 168–72.

19

Captain Hülsen [Political Section of the General Staff in Berlin] to the Foreign Ministry

AS 1234   Berlin, 30 March 1917

A confidential agent working for us, who spent a few days in Switzerland on our behalf and returned here on 29 March 1917, reports the following:

'A large number of the Russians living in Switzerland wish to return to Russia. In principle, the Entente agrees with this plan, but those members of Russian revolutionary parties who favour an immediate peace are to be kept out of Russia by English pressure. Three such Russian revolutionaries were refused entry into France in the last few days, although they had been issued with passports by the Russian consulate in Bern. These Russian revolutionaries asked me, in confidence, to suggest to the German government that it should help them to reach Russia in spite of all this, and they made the following suggestion:

"The German government should approve an application which the Russians living in Switzerland would arrange to have made by the Swiss government, for these Russians (about 300 to 400) to be transported to Sweden in a special train, travelling through Germany because of the shortness of this route. Among these 300 to 400 Russians (of all parties) there would also be those unacceptable to the Entente. As soon as the German government agrees to the proposal, he (the confidential agent) should unobtrusively inform the relevant people in Switzerland, so that they could begin to take the necessary steps with the Swiss government. (See the enclosed newspaper cutting.[1]) The basic conditions demanded for the success of the operation seemed to be speed of execution and the arousing of as little attention as possible in Switzerland. It would not be advisable to make any conditions as to those travelling on the train, such as excepting those liable for military service. It was considered advantageous to Germany to bring out the members of Lenin's party, the Bolsheviks, who were about forty in number. Among them were Lenin and Rjasanov in Bern, and Semjonov, Grigoriev, Abranov, Dora Dolin, and Marie Gutstein in Zürich. The fact that twenty to thirty so-called 'revolutionary patriots' and Mensheviks who were in favour of continuing the war would travel through at the same time seemed unimportant, as they would get back to Russia in any case, with the aid of the Entente." '

A decision on this proposal is humbly requested here.[2] Our confidential agent is available for co-operation.

HÜLSEN

---

[1] An undated cutting from *Volksrecht* headed 'Party News. Return of political refugees to Russia.' The last sentence reads: 'Steps are being taken to organize a return to Russia. Address: S. Bagocky, Klusstrasse 30, Zürich.'

[2] Marginal note by Bergen: 'To be passed on to Pourtales. (Hülsen would be glad of early information.)'

20

The Minister in Bern to the Foreign Ministry

TELEGRAM NO. 568

AS 1242   31 March 1917, 1.15 a.m.
                                Received: 31 March, 5.20 a.m.

National Counsellor [*Nationalrat*] Grimm has told Federal
Counsellor Hoffmann, in the name of the Zürich Committee,
that Russian *emigrés*, most of whom are in favour of peace, have
asked to be allowed to return to Russia immediately. Negotiations with the Swedish government would waste valuable time.
Travel through the Entente countries was impossible, quite
apart from the danger from submarines, because the Entente
would only allow those *emigrés* to travel who were in favour of
continuing the war. After their return to Russia the *emigrés*
would work for the release of a number of German prisoners
from Russia.

   After a discussion with me, Herr Hoffmann advised Grimm
that representatives of the committee should make direct contact with me and should also send a telegram to Kerensky.
Grimm considers the latter move inadvisable, as he does not
trust Kerensky.

   A representative of the committee will probably approach me
tomorrow. I intend to inform him according to the terms of
telegram No. 348[1] and to instruct him immediately to present
lists of those travelling.

                                                   ROMBERG

                    [1] Document No. 17.

21

Memorandum by Ow-Wachendorff[1]

AS 1206   Berlin, 31 March 1917

A General Staff discussion on the subject of the transport of
Russian revolutionaries took place this afternoon. The following
were present: Capt. (Cavalry) Zürn, head of the Central Passport Office, Capt. Burmann (Imperial Intelligence Bureau,
East), and myself.

Burmann emphasized that the Intelligence Bureau East was only moderately interested in the undertaking, but that they would, in any case, like to be given the list of names as soon as possible.

Zürn explained that the objections of the General Staff were mainly based on the fact that it seemed doubtful whether the Finnish frontier authorities, which have English officials attached to them, would allow those elements who are against a continuation of the war to cross. It seems very questionable whether we shall achieve our aims. Above all, we should avoid compromising those travelling, before they leave, by showing too much eagerness to co-operate. There were only political objections to the transport of larger numbers. No selection was possible. One might, at the most, limit permission to travel to those not fit for military service. One would then still have the possibility of adding those elements acceptable to us.

It was thought desirable that an application should have been made by the Swiss government. (See letter from the Political Section.[2]) Zürn was afraid that it could later be used against us if we were suddenly to send all these restless elements up to Sweden without any request from the Swiss. The Swiss had already made an official application in the summer of 1915 for the return to Russia of Russians with no means of support.

Ow.

[1] Legation Secretary Hans-Hartmann von Ow-Wachendorff.
[2] Document No. 19.

22

The Minister in Copenhagen to the Foreign Ministry

TELEGRAM NO. 528

AS 1273

2 April 1917, 3.13 a.m.
Received: 2 April, 5.45 a.m.

Had detailed discussion with Scavenius about the situation in Russia. The Minister rates the political significance of the Socialist Skobolev's inflammatory speeches lower than the press of the Entente countries might lead one to believe. Nevertheless, Scavenius does see in them a sign that the English are also in contact with the extremist Socialist circles.

In face of the Russian revolution, we can, in my opinion, adopt one of two attitudes:

Either we are both militarily and economically in a position to continue the war effectively until the autumn. In that case it is essential that we try now to create the greatest possible degree of chaos in Russia. To this end, any patently apparent interference in the course of the Russian revolution should be avoided. In my opinion, we should, on the other hand, make very effort surreptitiously to deepen the differences between the moderate and the extremist parties, for it is greatly in our interests that the latter should gain the upper hand, since a drastic change would then be inevitable and would take forms which would necessarily shake the very existence of the Russian empire. However, even if the moderate wing should remain in power, I could not imagine a transition to normal conditions taking place without considerable turmoil. Nevertheless, I think that it would be preferable, from our point of view, to back the extremist element, as this would be a more thorough way to work and would lead more quickly to some conclusion. In all probability, we should, in about three months time, be able to count on the disintegration having reached the stage where we could break the power of the Russians by military action. If we were now to launch a premature offensive, we should only give all the various centrifugal forces a motive for uniting and even, perhaps, lead the army to rally in its fight against Germany.

If, on the other hand, we are not in a position to continue the war until the end of this year with any likelihood of success, then we should try to achieve a *rapprochement* with the moderate parties now in power and to convince them that if they insist on continuing the war, they will merely be doing the work of the English for them, opening the gates to reaction, and thus jeopardizing even such freedom as they have won. As an additional argument, it should be pointed out to the Miliukovs and the Guchkovs that, in view of the uncertainty of the position in Russia, the English might attempt to reach an agreement with us, at the expense of the Russians.

BROCKDORFF-RANTZAU

2 3

The Minister in Copenhagen to the State Secretary

AS 1311   2 April 1917

Dear State Secretary,

I am writing this personal letter to Your Excellency today because I regard the acute situation which has recently arisen, and particularly the development of affairs in Russia, as so important to the ultimate decision regarding the form of our entire future policy, that I consider radical decisions to be inevitable if we are to assure ourselves success at the eleventh hour.

Your Excellency knows that I am not a hack, nor an idolater of the infamous *verbi magistri*. I have formed my own independent opinions and I believe that, in view of the respectful friendship which I feel for you and of the unconditional confidence which you have always shown in me, I now have a right to make myself heard.

My request is that you be kind enough personally to receive Dr. Helphand, who will be arriving in Berlin tomorrow evening (Tuesday). I am well aware that his character and reputation are not equally highly esteemed by all his contemporaries, and that your predecessor [Jagow] was especially fond of whetting his sharp tongue on him. In answer to this, I can only assert that Helphand has realized some extremely positive political achievements, and that, in Russia, he was, quite unobtrusively, one of the first to work for the result that is now our aim. Certain things, perhaps even everything, would be different now if Jagow had not totally ignored his suggestions two years ago!

The connexions which Helphand has in Russia could now, in my opinion, be decisive to the development of the whole situation. Moreover, he is also in such close contact with the Social Democrats in Germany, Austria, and Scandinavia that he could influence them at any time.

He is genuinely grateful to Your Excellency, as he knows that he has your intercession to thank for his acceptance into the German state at a time when his position was more than precarious, and he now feels himself to be a *German*, not a Russian, in spite of the Russian revolution, which should have brought about his rehabilitation. I therefore ask you to give him a hearing, since I am convinced that, properly handled, he could be extremely useful, not only in the decision of questions of international politics, but also in the internal politics of the Empire.

I have no need to emphasize that I am by no means in agreement with all his interpretations, but I think that we should nevertheless make use of powers such as his where we have need of them.

Your Excellency will understand the motives which led me to write this letter.

I have nothing further to add, except *that Helphand has never once suggested that I should recommend him to Your Excellency*, and that I only decided to write this letter a few hours ago, i.e. at 10 o'clock at night, because I happened to find out that an extra courier is travelling to Berlin tomorrow morning. In view of this, I must also ask you to forgive the fact that this letter was drafted in haste and may bear the outward signs of its hurried writing.

Yours, &c.
BROCKDORFF-RANTZAU

24

The Under State Secretary to the Minister in Bern

TELEGRAM NO. 380

AS 1242   Berlin, 2 April 1917

According to information received here, it is desirable that transit of Russian revolutionaries through Germany take place as soon as possible, as the Entente has already begun to work against this move in Switzerland. I therefore recommend all possible speed in your discussions with representatives of the committee.

BUSSCHE

25

The Minister in Bern to the Foreign Ministry

TELEGRAM NO. 601

AS 1288

3 April 1917
Dispatched: 4 April, 9.45 a.m.
Received: 4 April, 11.35 a.m.

In reply to telegram No. 380.

Although I have made our willingness to co-operate known to the *emigrés* through various channels, and although I have repeatedly been warned to expect a visit from a representative, nobody has yet contacted me, apparently because the *emigrés* are afraid of compromising themselves in Petrograd. Some of them definitely want to wait for instructions from the government in Petrograd or from the Soviet; others still seem uncertain as to whether or not they wish to avail themselves of our offer. I do not think that we can do anything but wait. Perhaps German Socialists could also sound the *emigrés*.   ROMBERG

26

The Under State Secretary to the Minister in Bern

DISPATCH NO. 302

AS 1234

Berlin, 4 April 1917

I beg to enclose herewith a copy of a letter from the Deputy General Staff, dated 30 March on the question of the transit through Germany of the Russian revolutionaries in Switzerland, for Your Excellency's information.[1]

The Deputy General Staff has been informed by us that Your Excellency is authorized to tell the representative of the Zürich Committee of the Russian revolutionaries the conditions imposed by the army for their journey through Germany.

BUSSCHE

[1] See document No. 19.

27

The Minister in Bern to the Foreign Ministry

TELEGRAM NO. 603

AS 1301   4 April 1917, 5.35 p.m.
                                    Received: 4 April, 7.20 p.m.

In continuation of telegram No. 601.

Platten, the secretary of the Social Democratic party, came to see me on behalf of a group of Russian Socialists and, more particularly, of their leaders, Lenin and Zinoviev, to voice a request that a number of the most important *emigrés*, twenty to sixty at the most, be allowed to travel through Germany immediately. Platten states that matters in Russia are taking a turn dangerous to the cause of peace, and that everything possible should be done to get the Socialist leaders here to Russia as soon as possible, as they have considerable influence there. Unfortunately, he said, many of the *emigrés* had no identity documents and, except for Lenin and Zinoviev, they were very anxious that their names should not be mentioned at all. Apart from this, they were prepared to submit to any conditions, such as travelling through without any stops and in sealed or even shuttered compartments. However, they did insist that none of them be left behind, that their carriage be assured extra-territorial rights, and that each of them be accepted regardless of his position for or against continuation of the war. For their part, they promised to make efforts in Russia to secure the release of a number of German prisoners. Platten, who wants to travel to Stockholm to set up an information service, would join up with the *emigrés* and would be prepared personally to guarantee each one of those travelling and to provide them with an authorization from [*one word garbled*]. This authorization should, if possible, contain no names. Platten could take the *emigrés* to the frontier together with a German official, and could take them through the frontier post one by one.

   Since their immediate departure would be greatly in our interests, I urgently recommend that permission should be granted at once, accepting the conditions laid down. Taking into account the suspicious nature of the Russians, who would not at first believe in the possibility of safe transit, together with the ruthless counter-activities of the Entente and the differences of opinion among the *emigrés* themselves, there would otherwise be a considerable danger of their allowing their decision to be altered again. If we show them unreserved confidence, we shall put them into a friendly frame of mind. I would consider it especially helpful that we should show our confidence in the Swiss Socialists by accepting their guarantee as a sufficient one. This would place us high in their estimation and would, I hope, enable us to establish a permanent relationship which would be extremely useful for maintaining connexions with Russia. Platten admits himself that there are two sides to the question of the justification and the logic of the conditions laid down by the *emigrés* for their journey. He said that they believed that they had, in this way, insured themselves against being compromised in Russia, and that, after laboriously reaching agreement, one should not reopen any discussion. Their departure should take place not later than Friday. Finally, Platten regards it as quite impracticable to consider the possibility of so-called Social Patriots, i.e. opponents of peace, presenting themselves for the journey. Please telegraph at least provisional instructions as to whether or not the Russians should hold themselves in readiness for Friday.

ROMBERG

28

The Minister in Bern to the Foreign Ministry

TELEGRAM NO. 607

AS 1302

4 April 1917
Dispatched: 5 April, 1.00 a.m.
Received: 5 April, 3.20 a.m.

In continuation of telegram No. 603.

National Counsellor Grimm has told Federal Counsellor Hoffmann that arrangements would be made for representatives of the Petrograd revolutionary committee to meet *emigrés* from Switzerland in Stockholm. He added that, in the interests of peace, it was also desirable that German Socialists (not, of course, followers of Scheidemann, but more moderate elements of the workers' community, such as Kautzky) should see Mehring[1] in Stockholm, in order to discuss peace. Grimm had gone on to remark, with a smile, that there was no risk for the

German government in this, since the Germans were a long way from being ripe for a revolution.

Hoffmann says that, although Platten is a representative of the most radical body of opinion, he has heard nothing else unfavourable of him.

ROMBERG

---

[1] Franz Mehring, German revolutionary Marxist, historian of the German Social Democracy, editor of *Leipziger Volkszeitung* and *Die neue Zeit*.

29

The State Secretary to Freihern von Lersner, the Foreign Ministry Liaison Officer at General Headquarters

TELEGRAM NO. 549

AS 1148   Berlin, 5 April 1917

According to information from Bern, departure of Russian *emigrés* in Switzerland is possibly imminent.

Request discussion with High Command of the Army as to whether it might not be advisable to give charge of journey through Germany to a tactful officer with political understanding, whose choice could perhaps be influenced by High Command of the Army.

It seems politically desirable that, while of course strictly observing all safety measures considered necessary in military quarters, all inconveniences which might unnecessarilly distress the *emigrés* be avoided as far as possible.

Further details of the organization of the journey will be agreed here with the Deputy General Staff.

ZIMMERMANN

30

The Under State Secretary to the Minister in Bern

TELEGRAM NO. 394

AS 1301   Berlin, 5 April 1917

In answer to telegram No. 603.[1]

General Staff agrees. Frontier-crossing at Gottmadingen. Understanding officer will take charge of train from Gottmadingen to Sassnitz. Hand-over at Gottmadingen by official of Foreign Service to be chosen there. No passport formalities of any kind at frontier-crossing. Luggage will be sealed. Safe transit guaranteed. German Trade Union leader Janson, a Socialist, will probably join train at Gottmadingen.

For technical reasons maximum number to travel sixty.

Further details of time of travel follow. Provisionally two second-class express carriages will be ready at Gottmadingen on Saturday evening.

BUSSCHE

[1] Document No. 27.

31

The Minister in Bern to the Chancellor

REPORT NO. 970

AS 1317   5 April 1917

I have the honour to present the enclosed draft of the conditions for the passage of Russian *emigrés* from Switzerland to Stockholm, given me by Herr Platten.[1]

ROMBERG.

Enclosure:

Basis for discussions concerning the return of *emigrés* to Russia.

1. I, Fritz Platten, will conduct the carriage carrying political *emigrés* wishing to travel to Russia, through Germany, bearing full responsibility and personal liability at all times.

2. All communication with German organizations will be undertaken exclusively by Platten, without whose permission absolutely nobody may enter the carriage, which will be locked at all times.

The carriage will be granted extra-territorial rights.

3. No control of passports or persons may be carried out either on entering or on leaving Germany.

4. Persons will be allowed to travel in the carriage absolutely regardless of their political opinions or their attitude towards the question of the desirability of war or peace.

5. Platten will buy tickets at the normal tariffs for those travelling.

6. As far as possible the journey shall be made without stops

and in a through train. The *emigrés* may not be ordered to leave the carriage, nor may they do so on their own initiative. The journey may not be interrupted except in case of technical necessity.

7. Permission to make the journey is granted on the basis of an exchange of those travelling for Germans and Austrians imprisoned or interned in Russia.

8. The negotiator and those travelling undertake to exert themselves, publicly and especially among the workers, to see that this condition is fulfilled.

9. The time of departure from the Swiss frontier for the Swedish frontier, which should be as soon as possible, shall be agreed immediately.

Bern–Zürich, 4 April 1917
FRITZ PLATTEN

[1] Cf. F. Platten, *Die Reise Lenins durch Deutschland*, Berlin, 1924, pp. 29–30.

32

The Minister in Bern to the Foreign Ministry

TELEGRAM NO. 619

AS 1322   6 April 1917, 8.00 p.m.
Received: 6 April, 10.25 p.m.

In reply to telegram No. 394.[1]

Platten reports about twenty members of Lenin's party ready to leave.

However, it is still possible that important Social Revolutionaries (the party of Weiss)[2] may join them. As yet, however, agreement with them has not been possible, and it is very doubtful whether the discussions with them can be finished in time. There is therefore an urgent desire that the journey be postponed until Sunday night, as great value should be laid on the participation of the Social Revolutionaries because of the important role that they played in the outbreak of the revolution. The simultaneous appearance of the leaders of both parties in Russia would make a deep impression and would considerably further active work for peace. I therefore urgently recommend that this wish be fulfilled and the journey be postponed until Sunday night.

The *emigrés* ask whether we could not, before their departure, make private representations to the Swedish government to secure their entry into Sweden. Herr Platten, who is to accompany the *emigrés*, requests that arrangements be made to ensure that he encounters no difficulties on his return journey from Stockholm to Switzerland.

Each of the *emigrés* has about three baskets by way of luggage, and they wish to travel third class, as many of them are without means and cannot pay the higher fare. Free travel is not to be recommended, and any obviously preferential treatment is also to be avoided. Furthermore, within German territory the *emigrés* must not communicate with any German except through Platten. Naturally the press must make no mention of the journey.

Please inform station at Gottmadingen of fare.

I urgently request instructions by telegram about postponement of journey. Answer must reach here not later than 10 o'clock tomorrow, Saturday.

ROMBERG

[1] Document No. 30.
[2] Weiss was the cover name of Zivin. See document No. 13.

33

The Under State Secretary to the Minister in Bern

TELEGRAM NO. 401

AS 1317   Berlin, 7 April 1917

In reply to report No. 970.[1]

Platten's conditions accepted except Clause 2, as proposal for journey was agreed after request from German Trades Unions, on whose behalf Janson will accompany the carriage.[2]

BUSSCHE

[1] See document No. 31.
[2] Marginal note: 'A copy humbly sent for information to Political Section of the General Staff, Berlin, for the attention of Capt. Hülsen.'

34

The State Secretary to the Minister in Stockholm

TELEGRAM NO. 480

AS 1322   Berlin, 7 April 1917

A number of Russian revolutionaries in Switzerland (exact number not yet decided) is to be given permission to travel through Germany in order to return to Russia via Sweden. They will be accompanied by the secretary of the Swiss Social Democratic party, Platten. Provisionally, they will probably arrive at Sassnitz on Wednesday, 11 April.

Please make the necessary arrangements with the Swedish government, in confidence.

Report their attitude by telegram.

                                              ZIMMERMANN

35

The Minister in Bern to the Foreign Ministry

TELEGRAM NO. 631

AS 1349   8 April 1917
                              Dispatched: 9 April, 1.00 a.m.
                               Received: 9 April, 4.10 a.m.

In reply to telegram No. 401.[1]

The *emigrés* expect to encounter extreme difficulties, even legal prosecution, from Russian government because of travel through enemy territory. It is therefore essential to their interests that they be able to guarantee not to have spoken with any German in Germany. Platten will explain this to Janson. It is absolutely essential also that the German press ignore the affair as long as it is not discussed abroad. If discussion becomes unavoidable, it should not add any commentary and, above all, should not pin any hopes on the affair such as might compromise the *emigrés*. On no account should Swiss role of mediation be mentioned.

Departure is to take place tomorrow according to plan. At least twenty-nine, possibly up to thirty-seven, Russian members of various groups of the Lenin wing will travel. It is still uncertain whether or not Social Revolutionaries will travel.

ROMBERG.

¹ Document No. 33.

36

The Minister in Copenhagen to the Foreign Ministry

TELEGRAM NO. 560

AS 1364   9 April 1917, 9.50 a.m.
                              Received: 9 April, 11.50 a.m.

Dr. Helphand has requested to be informed immediately of the arrival in Malmö or Sassnitz of the Russian refugees travelling from Switzerland through Germany. Helphand wishes to meet them in Malmö.
Please telegraph information immediately.¹

BROCKDORFF-RANTZAU

¹ Reply: Telegram No. 260, Berlin, 10 April. 'Russian *emigrés* from Switzerland will arrive Sassnitz at noon Wednesday. Zimmermann' (WK 2 secr, volume 32). In Radek's contribution to Platten's pamphlet *Die Reise Lenins durch Deutschland* (Berlin, 1924), p. 66, Radek wrote: 'In Stockholm Parvus tried to see Lenin in the name of the Central Committee of the German Social Democrats; Ilyich not only refused to see him, but asked me, Vorovski and Hanecki, together with Swedish comrades, to record this attempt.' Radek and Hanecki were the two closest contacts of Helphand's among the Bolsheviks.

37

The Minister in Bern to the Foreign Ministry

TELEGRAM NO. 634

AS 1357   9 April 1917, 2.05 p.m.
                              Received: 9 April, 4.05 p.m.

In continuation of telegram No. 631.¹

I wish to emphasize again that *emigrés* have taken no steps to procure permission to travel in Sweden and therefore rely absolutely on the action requested by us.

ROMBERG

¹ Document No. 35.

38

The Minister in Munich to the Foreign Ministry

TELEGRAM NO. 63

AS 1363   9 April 1917, 4.30 p.m.
                                  Received: 9 April, 7.45 p.m.

May I suggest to Your Excellency that I should sound Adolph
Müller[1] to see if he would be prepared to establish contact with
Russian Socialists in Scandinavia, on the spot. As I am not certain that he would accept, I should, for the moment, speak of
the matter only as if it were an idea of my own.

TREUTLER

[1] Müller was a Social Democrat deputy from Munich and a friend of Helphand.
Shortly after the war, he became the German Minister in Bern.

39

The Under State Secretary to the Minister in Bern

TELEGRAM NO. 413

AS 1357   Berlin, 10 April 1917

In reply to telegram No. 634.[1]

Minister in Stockholm has been instructed to approach Swedish
Government on the subject of journey of Russian *emigrés*
through Sweden.

BUSSCHE

[1] Document No. 37.

40

The State Secretary to the Minister in Munich

TELEGRAM NO. 22

AS 1363   Berlin, 10 April 1917

In reply to telegram No. 63.[1]

Scheidemann and Ebert have travelled to Scandinavia with my
approval. The possibility of their meeting Müller does not seem

to me very desirable. In addition, I want to await the reports of these two on their impressions. I therefore recommend that you do not, for the moment, take any steps.   ZIMMERMANN

¹ Document No. 38.

41

The Minister in Stockholm to the Foreign Ministry

TELEGRAM NO. 600

AS 1382   10 April 1917, 4.20 p.m.
                                         Received: 10 April, 6.57 p.m.

In reply to telegram No. 480.¹
Government here permits transit through Sweden.

                                                        LUCIUS

¹ Document No. 34.

42

The State Secretary to the Minister in Bern

TELEGRAM NO. 417

AS 1382   Berlin, 11 April 1917

In continuation of telegram No. 413.¹

According to report of Imperial Minister in Stockholm, Swedish government permits transit of Russian *emigrés*.

                                                    ZIMMERMANN

¹ Document No. 39.

43

Memorandum by Ow-Wachendorf

AS 1393   Berlin, 11 April 1917

Herr von Hülsen informs me that the Russians' journey has so far been extremely harmonious. An officer in civilian clothes visited the carriage here while it was in transit. He stated that Platten had said, on behalf of the Russians, that they were very gratified with the co-operation shown by the German government. Ample food had been provided, though the Russians had only wanted little. In Berlin, milk had been made available for the children.

The Russians' train missed its connexion in Frankfurt, so that their carriage was somewhat delayed. The Russians will therefore have to spend the night at Sassnitz. Good accommodation has been assured them there, in a locked room.   Ow

44

Memorandum by Ow-Wachendorf

AS 1406   Berlin, 12 April 1917

Lersner has telephoned as follows:

1. His Majesty the Kaiser suggested at breakfast today that the Russian Socialists travelling through Germany should be given White Books and other literature, such as copies of the Easter Message and of the Chancellor's speech, so that they may be able to enlighten others in their own country.

2. In the event of the Russians being refused entry into Sweden, the High Command of the Army would be prepared to get them into Russia through the German lines.

3. The High Command of the Army would also be prepared to get those Russians who are still in Switzerland into Russia through our lines. A telegram on this matter follows.   Ow

45

The Minister in Copenhagen to the Foreign Ministry

TELEGRAM NO. 575

A 12165   13 April 1917
                        Dispatched: 14 April, 11.30 a.m.
                          Received: 14 April, 3.4 p.m.

Thirty-three Russian *emigrés* arrived at Malmö yesterday, were welcomed at Trelleborg by the Mayor of Stockholm, and immediately travelled on to Stockholm. They told their comrades that there were still a considerable number of Russian *emigrés* in Switzerland who had not been able to travel as their passport formalities had not been completed. Whether reason for this lies on German or Swiss side is not known. It appears urgent that this be hurried up. Russian revolutionaries who appeared at Malmö to welcome the *emigrés* said that it was absolutely essential that as many first-class agitators as possible should be available to counteract the efforts of Miliukov and Guchkov to continue the war.

Among the *emigrés* still in Switzerland there are several of the best-known agitators.

The Danish Socialist Borbjerg has been informed in Haparanda that he is being refused entry into Russia. This refusal apparently emanated from the provisional government in Petrograd and as a result of representations from England. Borbjerg is going to protest, and will probably try to join up with the thirty-three *emigrés*, who have already left Stockholm for Russia this evening.

BROCKDORFF-RANTZAU

46

The Minister in Bern to the Foreign Ministry

TELEGRAM NO. 663

AS 1456   14 April 1917, 11.45 p.m.
                          Received: 15 April, 4.46 a.m.

The Socialist National Counsellor Grimm has asked Federal Counsellor Hoffmann for his help in getting permission to travel to Stockholm and back. From Stockholm, he might possibly travel on to Petrograd. Grimm believes that his presence is necessary to counteract Branting's activities against peace, that it is essential that the opportunity to conclude a separate peace be exploited, and that general peace would then follow. Although Hoffmann is a personal opponent of Grimm, of whose character he has a poor opinion, Hoffmann is inclined to recommend that permission be granted. Although it is well known that Grimm has bitterly attacked us, he has nevertheless stood resolutely in opposition to war; he played a leading part at

Zimmerwald and at Kiental, and has close connexions with the extreme left in Russia and France and with the Liebknecht group. As far as his work for peace is concerned, Hoffmann considers him to be absolutely honest, and says that he is working to secure for the Proletariat the credit for having restored peace to the world. It must be added, however, that the Socialists in our government have no use for him.

Grimm made the same request to me personally today, expressing himself extremely intelligently.

He would like to achieve the following in Petrograd:

1. Procure permission, either official or at least from the Committee, for the Russian *emigrés* in Switzerland, especially the Social Revolutionaries, who would have great influence on the peasants, to return to Russia through Germany. Without a cover of this kind, they do not dare to make the journey.

2. Sound out the possibilities of peace, and, if possible, give us his impressions through the Swiss Legation in Moscow.

He said that action must be taken quickly, and that, in his opinion, moderate members of the German workers' community, such as Kautzky, Mehring, and Haase, should be given permission to have talks with Russians in Stockholm. He further believed that an official German counter-announcement should be made to the Lvov manifesto, announcing our renunciation of annexations and war reparations, in order to strengthen the peace party in Russia. I would add here that the Russian revolutionaries have warned us against making any announcement which could give the impression that we are gambling on the revolution resulting in Russian military disorganization. Thus, they say, the publication of the Kaiser's congratulations to Stochod, Field-Marshal Hindenburg's alleged statements that the revolution was serving his own ends, and statements in the press such as Reventlow's article in the *Deutsche Tageszeitung* of 12 April have all done incalculable damage.

Both Hoffmann and President Schulthess appear to be particularly nervous as a result of the American declaration of war, and they seem worried that the opportunity of making peace with the Russians might not be exploited. They suggest that we might perhaps renounce annexations in the East and satisfy ourselves with the creation of frontier states with guaranteed autonomy. In these circumstances, I feel that I should recommend that Grimm both be given permission to make and actually make his journey, even if our Socialists should express opposition. Since Grimm successfully organized the journey of

Lenin and his comrades, which was of great value to us, and since he has also lately been maintaining the attitude we would have him maintain in the Tagwacht and the Swiss National Council, it would be hard to understand if we were to try to prevent him from making this journey. As he is very ambitious, he would take it as a grave insult and would be in a position to do us a great deal of damage through his connexions with the revolutionary camp in every country. He asks for an assurance that he will be allowed to travel both ways unobstructed, taking a number of proclamations and other publications with him. I feel that we should allow him to enjoy the same treatment as the *emigrés* from Brussels. He can do no damage on the military side, and he may be decidedly useful politically. What is certain is that the Russian revolutionaries will listen to Grimm, a Swiss whom, as one of the men of Zimmerwald, they like and trust, rather than to German Socialists, especially those of Scheidemann's group.

I request a decision as soon as possible.   ROMBERG

47

The State Secretary to the Minister in Bern

TELEGRAM NO. 428

AS 1456   Berlin, 15 April 1917

In answer to telegram No. 663.

There is no objection to Grimm's passing through Germany on his journey in either direction. He should be requested to cross German frontier at Weil-Leopoldshöhe and to travel via Sassnitz or Warnemünde. Return journey by same route. The literature Grimm brings will not be touched. Please give Grimm letter of recommendation for frontier authorities. Request that you inform me by telegram of date of his entry into Germany.

ZIMMERMANN

48

The State Secretary to the Minister in Bern

TELEGRAM NO. 429

AS 1456   Berlin, 16 April 1917

In continuation of telegram No. 428.

Scheidemann and Ebert have given most earnest warnings
about Grimm, who, they say, is definitely pro-Entente. If,
therefore, Your Excellency has not yet carried out the commission concerned with Grimm's journey through Germany,
please do not do so.

ZIMMERMANN

49

The Minister in Bern to the Foreign Ministry

TELEGRAM NO. 672

AS 1494   16 April 1917
Dispatched: 17 April, 12.30 a.m.
Received: 17 April, 7.15 a.m.

In reply to telegram No. 429.

Commission had already been carried out. Both Federal Counsellor Hoffmann and I remain of the opinion that decision was
correct, especially as Prince Lvov has told Swiss Minister that
the departure of the *emigrés* from Switzerland was a considerable
embarrassment to him. It was due to Grimm that this departure
was possible. Grimm is certainly a severe opponent of the German government, as is well known, but he is no more pro-
Entente than, say, Haase or Ledebour. The Zimmerwald and
Kiental conferences, over which Grimm presided, aroused more
fear and opposition in France and England than anywhere else.
Grimm has made representations to Hoffmann expressly favour-
ing a separate peace with Russia. He told me today that the
Entente was spreading the rumour that we wanted a separate
peace with Russia so that we could throw ourselves upon France,
and that he was trying to counter this story. In the National
Council, Grimm tabled a motion, in opposition to the French

Swiss, proposing that, if Switzerland protested against German violations of Human Rights, she must make a similar protest to the Entente. After all this, Grimm can hardly follow any political line in Russia other than that which is in all probability being followed by Lenin, i.e. continuing efforts on the part of the revolutionaries, against the present government as against the last, to force peace.

It appears to me that Scheidemann and Ebert, with whom Grimm is on hostile terms, fear his interference from personal and party reasons. In my opinion, it is now our business to stir up Russian [*one word garbled*] with all available means, and, to do so, we should not reject the co-operation even of a man like Grimm, whatever his motives or views may be.

Since he is now going to make his journey in any case and has asked me what he could take to Russia, I request authority to tell him that [*one word garbled*] rest on the basis of today's Austro-German peace manifesto.[1]

ROMBERG

[1] The State Secretary to the Minister in Bern. Telegram No. 432, Berlin, 17 April 1917. 'Answer to the last sentence of telegram No. 672. I agree. Zimmermann' (WK 2 secr, volume 33).

50

The Minister in Copenhagen to the Foreign Ministry

TELEGRAM NO. 595

A 12381   17 April 1917, 1.35 a.m.
                                    Received: 17 April, 8.00 a.m.

In reply to telegram No. 250.[1]

For the Secretary of State.

Dr. Helphand has returned from Stockholm today, where he was negotiating with the Russian *emigrés* from Switzerland. He was summoned by telegram to Berlin by the executive committee of the Social Democrat Party. He will arrive tomorrow for a few days and will live in Keithstrasse 14, where he will await Your Excellency's invitation.[2]

BROCKDORFF-RANTZAU

[1] The Secretary of State to the Minister in Copenhagen, telegram No. 250. Berlin, 6 April 1917. 'Thank you for your letter [Document No. 23]. Unfortunately Helphand had left before I could see him. Zimmermann' (WK 2 secr, volume 32).
[2] Marginal note: 'Dr. Helphand received a letter of invitation.'

51

*The Foreign Ministry Liaison Officer at the Imperial
Court to the Foreign Ministry*

TELEGRAM NO. 551

A 12976   General Headquarters, 21 April 1917, 5.35 p.m.
Received: 21 April, 6.35 p.m.

High Command of the Army has following message for Political
Section of General Staff in Berlin:

'Steinwachs sent following telegram from Stockholm on
17 April 1917:

' "Lenin's entry into Russia successful. He is working exactly
as we would wish. Hence cries of fury of Entente Social Democrats in Stockholm. Platten was turned back by the English at
frontier, a fact which has aroused considerable attention here."

'Platten is distinguished Swiss Socialist leader who accompanied Russian revolutionaries from Switzerland through Germany to Stockholm, and who wanted to travel on to Petrograd.'

GRÜNAU

52

The Minister in Bern to the Foreign Ministry

TELEGRAM NO. 742

A 13733   27 April 1917, 12.45 p.m.
Received: 27 April, 1.47 p.m.

The secretariat of the organizing committee of the Russian
revolutionary *emigrés* in Zürich has asked me, through the intermediary of a reliable Swiss Social Democrat, to get permission
for its five members, Martov, Martin [*one syllable garbled*], Axelrod, Semkovski, and Astrov, together with their associates, to
travel through Germany to Sweden immediately, under the
same conditions as Lenin's group. Having failed in its efforts to
get a guarantee of travel through the Entente countries from the
provisional government, the committee has decided to throw
aside all its worries and considerations on the score of being

compromised. They are unconditionally in favour of immediate peace and, next to Lenin, are the most important revolutionaries here. The number of those to travel is not yet certain. I would tentatively suggest that Münzenberg, who was the subject of my telegram No. 722,[1] should accompany them, but that we should also arrange for a German military escort, as we did in the first case. A speedy decision of the principle is imperative, to prevent any contrary influences from making themselves felt. Date of journey would still have to be arranged with those taking part. The English are supposed to be detaining a ship carrying Russian *emigrés* back from America, and this story favourably influenced the decision of the committee here.

ROMBERG

[1] Telegram No. 722 in WK 2 secr, volume 34. The Minister in Bern to the Foreign Ministry, 24 April 1917. 'The Secretary of the International Union of Socialist Youth Organizations, Münzenberg, begs to be allowed to travel to Stockholm to a meeting of the Union, which is to take place shortly. A reliable confidential agent recommends approval, as Münzenberg is in favour of peace. Please telegraph instructions whether visa is to be granted. Romberg.'

53

The Minister in Bern to the Chancellor

REPORT NO. 1273

A 14332   30 April 1917

Platten, who had accompanied the Russian revolutionary Lenin and his followers on their journey through Germany, visited me today to thank me on their behalf for services rendered. Unfortunately Platten was prevented from accompanying his fellow travellers to Russia. He was stopped at the frontier by an English officer, who cancelled his entry permit.

Lenin, on the other hand, received a splendid welcome from his followers. It can be said that three-quarters of Petrograd workers are behind him. The propaganda among the soldiers is more difficult; the opinion seems to be widespread among them that we are going to attack them. It is not clear yet which course the revolution will take. Perhaps it will be enough to substitute several members of the Provisional Government, like Miliukov and Guchkov, by socialists. In any case it would be absolutely necessary to increase the number of the partisans of peace by an influx from abroad. It is therefore recommended that those emigrants who are prepared to leave should receive the same facilities as Lenin and his comrades. The greatest speed is recommended, as it is to be feared that the Entente will exercise pressure on the Swiss government to prevent their departure.

Platten said there were a number of Russian revolutionaries in Germany whose dispatch to Russia he recommended. From Platten's remarks it became clear that the emigrants lack the means for the conduct of their propaganda, while the means of their enemies are unlimited. The funds collected for them went mainly to the Social Patriots. I shall have an agent investigate the delicate question of whether it may be possible to let them have such means without offending them. In the meantime I would be grateful for telegraphic information about whether the revolutionaries are being supported in any other way.[1]

ROMBERG

[1] Marginal note by Pourtales: 'I have spoken to Romberg. With that, the last sentence of his dispatch was settled.'

54

The State Secretary to the Minister in Stockholm

TELEGRAM NO. 622

A 14209   Berlin, 1 May 1917

According to Telegraph Agency in Petrograd, there has been a demonstration of 'The Wounded and Maimed', supposedly attended by over 50,000 people, directed against Lenin and his followers and demanding that the war be continued.

Request further details as soon as possible.   ZIMMERMANN

55

The Minister in Stockholm to the Foreign Ministry

TELEGRAM NO. 742

A 14350   2 May 1917, 2.00 p.m.
                                                Received: 2 May, 6.56 p.m.

In reply to telegram No. 622.

Herr von Heidenstam considers that report is very likely true, as both the political line Lenin is pursuing and his peace propaganda are completely independent, and he is thus now in a position of violent opposition to the government. According to a report received today from the Telegram Bureau, he has been summoned before the Workers' Council for this reason.

There have been large demonstrations in favour of peace, led by students, in front of Kazan cathedral, at which violent speeches were made against England and the United States, and more moderate ones against France. The assassination of General Katshalinski is considered significant because he was a spokesman of the new government.

Anarchy is on the increase.   LUCIUS

56

The Counsellor of Legation in Bern to Minister Bergen

AS 1850   9 May 1917

Dear Herr von Bergen,

Herr von Romberg would be grateful for information as to whether your Russian connexions cover not only Lenin and his group, but also the leading Social Revolutionaries (Chernov and his colleagues). Should you yourself not be sufficiently informed on this point, Herr von Romberg would be grateful if you could make inquiries at once.

He is *extremely* anxious to have this information *as soon as possible*, and asks that you send it by telegram.[1]

Yours, &c.,
SCHUBERT

[1] Bergen's reply: Telegram No. 569; Berlin, 12 May. 'In reply to Schubert's private letter: I have no connexions with them. Bergen. Bussche' (WK 2 secr, volume 36).

57

Memorandum by the Military Attaché of the Legation in Bern

9 May 1917

The following report from Herr Baier on the subject of support for the peace movement in Russia, dated 4 May, has arrived from Chiasso:

I had the opportunity, in Zürich, of talking with various

different groups of the Russian *emigrés*. What I heard and saw there confirmed the reports which I made recently after my discussions with Dr. Shklovsky[1] and P. Axelrod, and added yet more information.

When I carefully sounded several leading representatives of different groups within the pacifist Socialist party, these men said that it was extremely desirable that systematic, intensive, and effective agitation for peace should be supported by some well-known, neutral comrades. After they had shown clear and, I might almost say, joyful willingness to accept financial support for the specific purpose of work for peace, I said that I, for my part, would be happy to grant considerable sums for such a noble, humanitarian, and internationalist aim. Moreover, the Russian revolution had made such a magnificent moral impression and had aroused such generous impulses that other persons of my acquaintance would be only too pleased to sacrifice large sums to support the Russian revolution by helping to achieve an immediate peace. These offers were all accepted with great pleasure. The common complaint was that the parties and groups opposed to the war had smaller financial means at their disposal than those supporting the war, who had the resources of the state in their control. The English gold played an important role, and the Entente was spending enormous sums on the support of the war-effort and on bribing influential people. It would therefore be all the more pleasing if large sums could be put at the disposal of those in favour of peace by wealthy comrades and friends. As far as peace is concerned, nearly all those with whom I spoke were less interested in a general peace concluded simultaneously with, and with the agreement of the other Entente powers, than in immediate peace *à tout prix*, that is, a separate peace with Germany and Austria. After this, the question of ways and means by which this support for peace propaganda should be got into Russia and put to its intended use produced a variety of detailed opinions which, for the sake of brevity, I shall summarize in a few sentences:

1. The personality of the donor would guarantee that the money came from an unobjectionable source.

2. The donor or the bearer of the money should be enabled, by official or semi-official recommendations, to cross the Russian frontier with it.

3. For the money to be immediately useful, ready cash would have to be available, not some kind of letters of credit which would be difficult to exchange and would attract attention.

Swiss currency could most easily, most efficaciously, and least obtrusively be turned into some liquid and useful form.

The question of distribution to the various parties, groups, and individuals who were to be granted shares of any subsidy for their agitation for peace, was already under discussion.

They all showed that there is willingness to accept support for the purpose in question and that, on the one hand, coming from me, the offer silenced all their doubts and objections, while it was clear, on the other hand, that my personal connexions with official personalities in government circles here were considered extremely advantageous to the practical execution of the project.

NASSE

¹ Grigorii Lvovich Shklovsky, a Bolshevik, in 1915 took part in the Bern Conference of the Bolshevik Organizations abroad, and was elected to this organization's committee; returned to Russia in time for the November revolution. In 1918 he returned to Switzerland with the Soviet diplomatic mission.

58

The State Secretary to the Minister in Stockholm

DISPATCH NO. 227

A 15080   Berlin, 9 May 1917

Dr. Helphand, who was well known in the Russian revolution of 1905 under the pseudonym 'Parvus', has done us a number of notable services in the course of the war, especially, working under the Imperial Minister in Copenhagen, in influencing the Danish trades unions in a direction extremely favourable to us. Since then, Dr. Helphand has been granted Prussian citizenship. He is travelling via Copenhagen to Stockholm, where he expects to arrive within the next few days, with the object of working for our interests at the impending Socialist congress. He will also try to establish contact with the Swedish trades unions.

I would ask Your Excellency to be friendly and helpful towards Dr. Helphand, who will call at the Legation, and to give him all possible assistance.

ZIMMERMANN

59

The Under State Secretary to the Minister in Stockholm and to the Minister in Bern

AS 1811   Berlin, 10 May 1917

1. TELEGRAM NO. 666

Please let loose, through your agent, agitation for publication of military and political agreements made with France and England by old régime in Russia before the war.

STUMM

2. TELEGRAM NO. 561

Please draw the attention of the *emigrés* returning to Russia, through suitable agents, to the idea that they should demand from their government the publication of agreements made by the old Russian régime with England and France.

STUMM

60

The Minister at The Hague to the Chancellor

REPORT NO. 2026

A 16533   18 May 1917

Among the numerous Russians who are at present living in Holland—there are about 2,600 civilian refugees and 300 soldiers from German prisoner-of-war camps in Rotterdam alone—there is considerable dissatisfaction with the Russian authorities here, and a certain section of these people is in sympathy with the Russian revolution.

The opportunity has just arisen to make contact with a representative of this last section, and, on this occasion, as had seemed likely, it appeared that the present situation could probably be very profitably exploited for the advancement of our political aims.

The personality in question is a certain Vladimir Futran. This man would appear to have escaped from a prisoner-of-war camp at Döberitz. He is a revolutionary of Lenin's group, and, although he has had no very complete education, is an intelligent man.

Whether or not, or to what extent his revolutionary opinions are genuine, what motives underlie his action, and how far he is governed by self-seeking and material aims, it is of course impossible to say so soon. On the whole, he gives the impression of being a political fanatic with a desire to avenge some injustice suffered by himself or his class.

In the course of the first discussion, which took place absolutely privately and on uncommitted territory between him and Dr. Wichert, Futran developed some very useful ideas which, after taking our contribution into account, add up to something like the following plan:

1. Futran, together with some comrades sharing his opinions, is founding a 'Russian Peace League in Holland'. This league is openly to make propaganda in favour of the immediate beginning of peace negotiations by the Russians. It will therefore also have to work against English politics directed at continuing the war, against English imperialism, and against the English activities in Russia. This would have to be done in the Dutch press, and also elsewhere with leaflets and other literature printed both in Dutch and in Russian.

2. Those of the revolutionary agitators among the Russians here who are not needed for the action planned for this country —about ten so far—should, after all necessary safety measures had been taken, be allowed to travel to Stockholm for the conference, from where they could perhaps go on to Russia. These men would have to maintain contact with the 'Peace League' in Holland and provide it with material for its activities.

3. The 'Russian Peace League' could be made to serve as a starting-point for agitation among the Russian prisoners of war in Germany and Austria. Agitation of this nature could be so directed as to help those elements in Russia which appear useful to us at the moment, for example Lenin's group. On the other hand, it could equally well be undertaken less specifically, simply with a view to the role which will be played by the two million returning Russian prisoners of war. The method of sowing the seeds of agitation in the camps, of spreading them, and of watching over them would have to be carefully considered. For the moment, it does not appear necessary to make any definite detailed decision.

Meanwhile, Futran has delivered the first evidence of his

abilities as a journalist and propagandist. The article from the *Nieuwe Rotterdamsche Courant* [14 May 1917], which I humbly enclose, ending in a violent attack on England and at once re-printed in The Hague newspaper *Het Vaderland* [15 May], is the immediate product of the relationship set up between the author and ourselves.

Herr Futran is now being encouraged further, while at the same time being kept sufficiently dependent to allow us to em-bark, entirely as we please, on those aspects of the projected plan which are mentioned above.

If he is successful in winning himself a corner in the Dutch press on the strength of the very promising beginning marked in the enclosure, and in bringing his 'Peace League' into a position of esteem, then the matter would certainly be worth active sup-port. However, the details given above probably open the way to much more effective undertakings.

In view of this situation, I humbly recommend that Your Excellency give me authority to seize the opportunity offered here, and that you be kind enough to grant the necessary funds for the agitation begun by Herr W. Futran among his com-patriots in Holland (which should, if possible, be continued on the largest of scales), and also for his work in the Dutch press. It is hardly likely that more than 600 guilders will be needed for the first month, which should be regarded as a probationary period, but the movement may soon take on an unexpectedly large form. For this reason, I would be grateful to have a larger sum, say 3,000 to 4,000 guilders, at my disposal from the start.[1]

I shall have the honour to report to Your Excellency, at suit-able intervals, about the further development of the whole affair, and about the forms it assumes after the probationary month.

ROSEN

---

[1] This request was granted by telegram No. 299 from the State Secretary to The Hague on 25 May 1917: 'In reply to report A 2026. You may put 3,000 guilders at Futran's disposal. Zimmermann' (WK 2 secr, volume 38).

61

The State Secretary to the Foreign Ministry Liaison Officer at the Imperial Court

TELEGRAM NO. 1010

AS 2117   Berlin, 29 May 1917

The Minister in Sofia telegraphed as follows on 28 May under No. 257.

'On the occasion of my last visit, M. Radoslavov[1] expressed concern as to Kerenski's effectiveness, and said that, if matters continued to develop in this way, we should have to consider whether to go on being mere spectators or whether rather to launch into an offensive.

'Radoslavov spoke in the same vein to my Austro-Hungarian colleague, who told me that he agreed with M. Radoslavov's opinion and said that—given, of course, that the necessary forces are available—we should set the Russians a time-limit, after which we should cease to regard our peace guarantees as binding.

'When I questioned him, Dobrovich, the head of the Privy Council, who can presumably be taken to speak for His Majesty the King, recommended the adoption of an energetic line, saying that the Russians had now been left in peace for long enough and were apparently not to be tempted by the offer of a separate peace.

'King Ferdinand and M. Radoslavov will probably raise this question on the occasion of their impending visit.'

I am still of the opinion that there must be no offensive, as an offensive would weld all the divergent elements in Russia together in their fight against us. On the other hand, it seems to me worth considering whether we should not for the moment break off discussions between the front-line trenches, telling the Russians that the reason for this is that we can no longer expect any success from these discussions, now that the provisional government, under the influence of the French and the English, has decided to continue the war. The Russians would have to be told this in such a way that they could not possibly conclude that we were intending to open an offensive.   ZIMMERMANN

[1] The Bulgarian Prime Minister and Minister of Foreign Affairs.

62

The State Secretary to the Minister in Bern

TELEGRAM NO. 658

AS 2198   Berlin, 3 June 1917

In answer to telegram No. 967.[1]

Secret reports show that the governments of the Entente countries continue to show great anxiety about Russia. The spread
of the idea of peace has not been stopped even by the latest—
and only temporary—consolidation of the provisional government. The despairing advances of the Russian troops cannot
dissimulate the growing disorganization and unwillingness to
fight of the Russian army. Lenin's peace propaganda is growing
steadily stronger, and his newspaper *Pravda* already prints
300,000 copies. Work in the armament factories is either at a
standstill, or has sunk to very low production figures. The transport crisis continues to grow more acute and, as a result, the
supply of food to the towns and the army is suffering. There is
therefore absolutely no possibility of the Entente receiving help
from that quarter.

ZIMMERMANN

[1] Telegram No. 967 of 1 June 1917. An Italian agent of the mission in Bern
wanted to know whether the reliance on Russia of the Entente countries was
justified (AS 2198 in WK 2 secr, volume 39).

63

The Minister in Stockholm to the State Secretary

AS 2433   15 June 1917

Dear State Secretary,

Scheidemann[1] was yesterday received by the Minister, who,
for his part, also wished to make his acquaintanceship. I saw
Herr Lindman immediately afterwards, and he expressed his
great respect for this 'wise and intelligent man'. Lindman is of
the opinion that the most important thing is that the discussions
should go on; whether in Petrograd or here, or with Scheidemann's group or the minority, he says, is only of secondary importance. I am now of the opinion, shared by Janson, Baake,

and others, that it is essential to try to bring our Socialists into direct contact with the Russian representatives. It does not even really matter if, as is only natural, the Russians would rather talk with Kautzky, &c. Since, as was to be expected, Branting has behaved with such hostility at the discussions, it would be advisable to exclude him entirely from future discussions engaged in by the minority party. It will not be difficult to make the Russian Socialists, and our own, understand that Branting is not really a Socialist at all but a bourgeois in disguise, and that he has a lot of money, likes to drink champagne, and leads a dissipated life. The Russians and the Germans here can convince themselves of this any day.

Gratifying news is that a representative of the Russian Workers' and Soldiers' Council has already arrived. He is called Weinberg. Our Socialists have therefore postponed their departure. Presumably a small delegation will stay here in any case. When the English and the French now see that we are really negotiating with the Russians, and doing so directly, without the help of neutrals, they will, in my opinion, grow extremely uneasy and will do everything they can still to take part in the conference, in spite of everything. I refuse to believe that the French government will succeed, in the long run, in preventing its Socialists from taking part in the discussions, here or in Petrograd, by refusing them passports. The strikes in France are already thoroughly revolutionary in character, and the property-owning classes are now growing really anxious. Wallenberg, with whom I always maintain contact because of his excellent connexions with high banking circles in London and Paris, always says that the Frenchman would rather be shot than parted from his money. In Lindman's opinion, the most unfavourable factor is the situation in England. Lloyd George simply does not care about the fact that a continuation of the war might also bring about the revolution and sweep away the monarchy. In fact Lindman even believes that this is Lloyd George's aim, not only in England, but in all the other monarchies as well.

Your Excellency will receive detailed information about events here from Janson. Even though the preliminary negotiations have not achieved much, I nevertheless believe that the stone will now go on rolling and that we shall make direct contact with the Russians, without Branting's being able to disturb our people here. It is very fortunate that Troelstra is now also going to Petrograd. The representative of the Petrograd Telegraph Agency, Studiakov, whom I knew well in Petrograd as correspondent for the *Vossische Zeitung*, has recently been trying to contact me. For the moment, however, I have deliberately not seen him.

Yesterday there were fairly definite reports of the growth of the revolutionary movement in Italy circulating here. However, I have not yet been able to ascertain whether there is any truth in them. In Wallenberg's opinion, it is only a matter of time before the revolution breaks out there.

The Social Democratic deputy Lindblad, who had breakfast with me yesterday, will have the honour of speaking to Your Excellency about the coal question which Janson also discussed in his personal letter. I regard an arrangement of this kind as so important, from a political point of view, that, in our discussion with Janson yesterday, I firmly rejected the objections raised by Dr. Warburg, who only considers matters from the commercial angle. This business must go through, quite regardless of whether or not it suits Herr Boetzow and whatever the other people are called.

Yours, &c.,
Lucius

N.B. Huysmanns has received a telegram from Petrograd, saying that representatives of the Workers' and Soldiers' Council will be arriving here at the end of the month as no agreement could be reached otherwise because of the poor communications.

[1] Scheidemann recorded his experiences at the Stockholm conference in his *Memoirs of a Social Democrat*, London, 1929, volume 2, chapter i, pp. 337–53.

64

Foreign Ministry to the Liaison Officer at General Headquarters

TELEGRAM NO. 358

A 20706   Berlin, 6 July 1917

In answer to telegram No. 947 of 17 June.[1]

Before their departure, Romanov and Tatarinov, who conducted the last convoy of Russian *emigrés* from Brussels, presented a list of eighteen more Russian Socialists who also wish to return home via Stockholm, but who could not travel with the first convoy for personal reasons. According to Romanov and Tatarinov, the majority of these people are also followers of Lenin.

An examination as to whether there are objections to the journey in individual cases will be made by the Political Department in Brussels.

Since it would seem desirable to return as many followers of Lenin as possible, we support the application. I therefore humbly request Your Excellency to procure the agreement of the High Command of the Army and to arrange for the necessary instructions to be given to the Central Passport Offices in Berlin and Brussels.

LANGWERTH-SIMMERN

¹ General Headquarters, 17 June: 'The Supreme Command communicates that Brussels has reported that the transport of Russian Socialists will arrive at Sassnitz on 17 June at noon. Courier for the transport: Lt. Rossbach. Lersner' (A 19724 in WK 2 secr, volume 41).

65

The Counsellor of Legation in Stockholm to the Chancellor

REPORT NO. 823

A 23125   11 July 1917

No. 7 of the Russische Korrespondenz *Prawda*¹ reports that no agreement was reached in the negotiations between the Russian Bolsheviks Ganecki, Vorovski, and Radek, and the German Social Democrats Haase, Ledebour, and Herzfeld. The Bolsheviks, who reject any suggestion of working with the 'Social Patriots', are shocked by the fact that the German left-wing Socialists should want to negotiate with the pro-Entente 'Social Patriots'. On this point, the newspaper makes the following comment:

'The participation of the German Social Patriots in this "Work for Peace" is, of course, very distasteful to them, but, in order to have the pleasure of meeting the fathers of the Russian offensive, they are prepared—under protest, of course —to accept even this misfortune. The Russian Workers would like to know what attitude the Spartacus group takes to this decision made by the Independents.'

According to reports from Petrograd in the newspapers here, and according to other sources, the influence of Lenin's group has unfortunately lessened. In a decision concerning a vote of confidence in the provisional government—a decision more or less bringing to an end the deliberations of the Workers' and Soldiers' Council—the Bolsheviks, reinforced by the internationalist Social Democrats and the Ukrainians, only raised 126 votes, while the majority was able to dispose of 543 votes. The waning of the Bolsheviks' influence must be seen as the result, partly of the offensive, and partly of the inordinate demands made by Lenin's group. These demands, of which the most extreme is the expropriation of the big capitalist concerns (especially of all banks and all the larger industrial and commercial undertakings) and the big landowners, aim at the detachment of all the various individual peoples from Russia and their formation into separate republics. It must be added, however, that, on the Ukrainian question, the Bolsheviks have somewhat changed their position, and that they now only demand a strong degree of autonomy for the Ukrainians, not their total detachment. *Pravda* for 28 June writes:

'The failure of the politics of the provisional government and its coalition cabinet grows more apparent from day to day. The "Universal Act" published by the Ukrainian Central Council and accepted by the All-Ukrainian Soldiers' Congress on 11 June, is documentary evidence of this failure.

'This act says: "The Ukrainian people should have the right to dispose of its own life in its own land, without detaching itself from Russia and without breaking away from the Russian state. Only our Ukrainian assembly has the right to promulgate laws guaranteeing order here in the Ukraine; laws concerned with the maintenance of order within the whole of the Russian state should be passed by the All-Russian Parliament."'

These are perfectly explicit words. They say, with all possible clarity, that the Ukrainian people does not at present wish to separate from Russia. It demands autonomy, but does not in any way dispute the necessity for or the sovereignty of the 'All-Russian Parliament'.

A remarkable thing is that the Petrograd Cossacks' Council has declared itself against the detachment of the Ukraine. Although the majority of Cossacks come from the Ukraine, and although they have always attached importance to a certain degree of autonomy, they nevertheless feel that they are historically an inseparable part of the whole Russian army. Moreover, they played such a decisive and, to them, glorious role in crushing the liberal and democratic elements in all earlier attempted revolutions, that one could hardly expect them to show genuine sympathy for the parties whose aim is to divide up Greater Russia.

I have the honour humbly to enclose a violent attack against the offensive from the Helsinki newspaper *Volna*, which accompanied the Korrespondez *Prawda*.   STOBBE

---

[1] Die russische Korrespondenz *Prawda*, was edited in German by Hanecki in Stockholm.

66

Memorandum for the State Secretary

AS 2840

Berlin, 17 July 1917

Dr. Helphand, who has returned from Stockholm, had a favourable impression of his various discussions with the Russian revolutionaries. He said that the influence of Lenin, and of the other groups working for a general peace, was continuing to grow, in spite of all the claims to the contrary made in the press of the Entente countries. The offensive had only taken place because the Americans and the English had made it a condition for the supply of money and raw materials, especially of cotton. The soldiers had only been won over to making the offensive by being told that they could see for themselves that the negotiations made since the outbreak of the revolution had not succeeded in bringing peace, whereas a successful offensive would lead quickly and surely to this result. Disappointment had already set in, and would result in a further softening-up of the army. This had already reached such a degree, even before the offensive, that the army, through the person of Brusilov, had said that the collapse of the armed forces could only be prevented by an immediate offensive. In addition to this, there was the poor harvest. The Russians living in Stockholm had claimed that only 30 per cent. of the area being farmed before the war was under cultivation now. Helphand regards this as an exaggeration, but thinks that the total could hardly, in fact, be more than 50 per cent.

Helphand also told me, after asking me to treat this information with the utmost confidence, that the Russians were not going to allow any discussion of the question of war-guilt at the congress which is beginning in Stockholm in the middle of August. They did not want to quarrel, but to do useful work for the preparation of peace. Similarly, they were not going to let themselves be drawn into any consideration of French wishes concerning Alsace-Lorraine, and they were hopeful that this question, too, might be got round. For the moment, however, care must be exercised to prevent the English from getting wind of the matter prematurely and thwarting the attendance of the French.

Helphand has been summoned for 6 p.m. today, in accordance with instructions.[1]

[1] Marginal note by Zimmermann: 'He told me the same. 17. 7.

67

The Chancellor to the Foreign Ministry Liaison Officer at General Headquarters

TELEGRAM NO. 1328

AS 2936

Berlin, 26 July 1917

With reference to telegram No. 52751 from Operational Department to Lieutenant-Colonel von Haeften, I request that General Ludendorff be told the following: Compliance with secret Order I a 4000 given to Eastern Command and Army Group Mackensen would mean a new offer of peace to Russia, or would at least be interpreted as such by Russian press and public opinion in Russia. I do not consider present moment suitable for such a step. If our counter-offensive is strong enough to make those now in power in Russia fear its continuation, then they, or in the event of their removal, their successors, will try to make contact with us of their own accord. If it is not strong enough, then these steps, which, in addition bear the stamp of extreme haste, will only have harmful effects. I should therefore be very grateful if the intended statement could be temporarily shelved, and if General Ludendorff could give me an opportunity to express an opinion before he formulates new principles for propaganda at the front. We must be very careful that the literature with which we are aiming to further the process of disintegration inside Russia does not achieve the directly opposite result.[1] This is especially true of the furtherance of separatist tendencies, which are falling into disrepute. For example, the Ukrainians still reject the idea of total secession from Russia. Any open intervention on our part in favour of an independent Ukrainian state would undoubtedly be exploited by the enemy in order to denounce the existing nationalist currents as German creations.

MICHAELIS

1 E. Vandervelde, who spent two weeks touring the Eastern front in June 1917, wrote in his *Three Aspects of Russian Revolution* (London, 1918, p. 134): 'It seems that this propaganda, while admirably organized and splendidly carried on has the same fault that we find in all German enterprises of this sort; it over-reaches its mark, and provokes finally, by its ponderous insistence, a psychological reaction which is the one result that its organizers failed to foresee.' Vandervelde also noticed the similarity between German propaganda and the views of the Bolsheviks, the Mensheviks, and the Internationalists (p. 133). Bruce Lockhart wrote in *The Two Revolutions* (London, 1957, p. 93): '. . . most of the Bolshevik propaganda, including Lenin's articles, which reached the Russian front was disseminated by the Germans, who, either with or without the connivance of Lenin, were able to buy the Bolshevik newspapers in Stockholm and reproduce them.'

68

The Minister in Copenhagen to the Foreign Ministry

TELEGRAM NO. 1044

A 26509

10 August 1917
Dispatched: 11 August, 12.40 a.m.
Received: 11 August, 5.45 a.m.

The Russian newspaper *Riech* for 20 July announced that two Germal General Staff officers called Schidicki and Luebers had told a Russian lieutenant, by the name of Jermolenko, that Lenin was a German agent. It also said that Jacob Fürstenberg and Dr. Helphand (Parvus) were German agents acting as intermediaries between the Bolsheviks and the Imperial government.

I consider it essential, first of all to discover whether these German General Staff officers, Schidicki and Luebers, in fact exist, and then, if at all possible, categorically to deny the report in *Riech*.

Riech also states that, according to a report telegraphed from Copenhagen, Haase, the German Social Democratic member of the Reichstag, said, in conversation with a Russian journalist, that Helphand was an intermediary between the Imperial government and the Russian Bolsheviks, and that he had transferred money to the latter.

I request information by telegram.

BROCKDORFF-RANTZAU

69

The Under State Secretary to the Minister in Copenhagen

TELEGRAM NO. 608

A 26509   Berlin, 18 August 1917

In answer to telegram No. 1044.

The suspicion that Lenin is a German agent has been energetically countered in Switzerland and Sweden at our instigation. Thus the impact of the reports on this subject supposedly made by German officers has also been destroyed.

The statement claimed to have been made by Haase has been denied.

BUSSCHE

70

The Legation in Copenhagen to the Foreign Ministry

TELEGRAM NO. 1074

A 27897   22 August 1917, 9.59 p.m.
Received: 23 August, 4.00 a.m.

For Deputy Erzberger and Counsellor Nadolny.

Wucherpfennig[1] reports:

Leitis travelling to Petrograd in next few days as courier for [Russian] Legation here. He will also take prosecution material for Lenin's trial. Bolshevik leader Radek still here. Report on his activities will be sent tomorrow. Goldberg's presence urgently required. If his departure delayed by passport difficulties, please send Parvus's pamphlets, as there is opportunity to dispatch them.

Meanwhile Meier Grossmann (Ruskie Viedomosti) has returned from Petrograd. He spoke with Savinko (Kerensky's 'Commissar for the Front') and with the Minister. Report will be sent after Goldberg's return.

Please inform Goldberg of the above.

LEGATION

[1] One of Erzberger's agents in Scandinavia. There is no mention of him in Erzberger's war memoirs, *Erlebnisse im Weltkrieg*, Stuttgart and Berlin, 1920.

71

The State Secretary to the Foreign Ministry Liaison Officer at General Headquarters

TELEGRAM NO. 1610

AS 3640   Berlin, 29 September 1917

For the information of the High Command of the Army.

The military operations on the Eastern front, which were prepared on a large scale and have been carried out with great success, were seconded by intensive undermining activities inside
Russia on the part of the Foreign Ministry. Our first interest, in
these activities, was to further nationalist and separatist endeavours as far as possible and to give strong support to the
revolutionary elements. We have now been engaged in these
activities for some time, and in complete agreement with the
Political Section of the General Staff in Berlin (Capt. von
Hülsen). Our work together has shown tangible results. The
Bolshevik movement could never have attained the scale or the
influence which it has today without our continual support.
There is every indication that the movement will continue to
grow, and the same is true also of the Finnish and Ukrainian
independence movements.

According to the most recent reports received here, the situation in Russia is that the country, whose economic life has been
shattered, and which is only just being held together by English
agents, could be expected to collapse as a result of any further,
fairly powerful shock. The very knowledgeable specialist in
Russian affairs at the Swedish Foreign Ministry has said that
the English influence depends on the rail connexion between
Petrograd and Haparanda, which is only capable of carrying
passenger traffic and mail.

The preparations for the Finnish rising are, as the High Command of the Army knows, busily under way and are being supported to a considerable extent. However, it is unlikely that they
can be maintained right through the winter if the Finnish hopes
in us are disappointed this autumn and the country is made dependent on Russia by the food shortage which must be expected
in the spring. On the other hand, in face of the weakness of the
Russians, we could expect the Finnish rising to break out now

and to reach a successful conclusion if we were to preserve Finnish confidence in us—a feeling very much in our interests— by occupying the Aaland Isles, which dominate the Gulf of Bothnia, and by forcing the Russian Army Command to withdraw some of the troops stationed in Finnland, by putting pressure on them at the front.

The occupation of the Aaland Isles would also be of the utmost political significance with regard to Sweden. Our enemies hope to deliver us a decisive blow by interrupting the export of Swedish ore, and are therefore making great efforts to alienate Sweden from us. The general situation in Sweden favours these efforts. The country is suffering acutely from a shortage of a number of commodities which the Entente is withholding from the Swedes, in retaliation for their strict observance, by contrast with the Norwegians and the Danes, of their neutrality. The Swedish people are being told that a government under Branting would procure all these goods, especially American oil, which is essential to the Swedish peasant in the long winter nights; and it is being suggested, in addition, that such a government could, with English aid, achieve the practical detachment of the Aaland Isles from Russia by winning the concession of a plebiscite. It has long been a Swedish wish to possess these islands, which command the entrance to Stockholm. Even if we were able to thwart the plans of the Entente in Sweden, the occupation of the Aaland Isles would so strengthen and secure our position against any possible reverses, that our enemies in the North would then have no further hope whatsoever.

In these circumstances, I wish to recommend that the question of occupying the Aaland Isles with German armed forces— and according to reports received here, this would have to be done not later than the first half of November—a question which is eminently important to our position in the East and the North and to the whole outcome of the war, should be carefully examined by the High Command of the Army.[1]   KÜHLMANN

[1] There are two replies to this telegram in Russland Nr. 63, Nr. 1 secr, volume 6. The first one, telegram No. 1455 of 1 October (AS 3715), from Grünau, concerns the question of the Aaland Islands only and gives Ludendorff's view that the occupation of the Islands was, for the time being, out of the question. Ludendorff maintained that the clearance of mines would take too long and would keep too large a part of the navy occupied. In the second telegram, No. 1493 of 6 October (AS 3761), Ludendorff acknowledges the undermining activities in Russia of the Foreign Ministry and of the Political Section of the Deputy General Staff, expresses thanks for the allocation of large amounts of money for it, and stresses the value of this work, especially in Finland. He shares the view that the occupation of the Aaland Islands would be of great political value to Germany, but could be accomplished only if the German lines of communication could run across Sweden.

72

The Minister in Stockholm to the Foreign Ministry

TELEGRAM NO. 1796

AS 4178

8 November 1917, 5.5 p.m.
Received: 8 November, 8.10 p.m.

For Bergen.

Please forward 2 millions of the War Loan for agreed purposes.
Riezler.

LUCIUS

Editorial note

One day after the Bolshevik seizure of power in Petrograd Bergen,
in the Foreign Ministry in Berlin, started testing his connexions with
the men now in power in Petrograd. He telegraphed to Vienna on
9 November, asking Helphand to visit him when he passed through
Berlin (AS 4182 in WK 2 secr, volume 51; all subsequent documents
referred to in this note are either in the series WK 2 secr or WK
11c secr).

On the same day, before Bergen's message reached him, Helphand
dispatched two telegrams, using the official channels of the Embassy
in Vienna. In the telegram to Copenhagen he requested an agent of
his to travel to Stockholm immediately and to let him know when he
was needed there. In the second telegram, Helphand asked his
friend Müller, the Social Democrat deputy at the time in Switzerland,
to meet him in Munich.

A few hours later, Bergen sent a cryptic telegram to Bern: 'In view
of the events in Russia Baier's journey to the North is desirable'
(AS 4180 in WK 2 secr, volume 51). On 11 November Romberg
replied that Baier could leave, if necessary, the same week, and that
Nasse, the military attaché in Berne, would go to Berlin to discuss
the matter with Bergen. Bergen gave his final consent for Baier's
journey on 22 November. (Cf. document No. 91.)

In the meantime, Helphand was being extremely elusive to his
official friends. It was at this time that the Foreign Ministry
and Helphand began to differ on the form the peace negotiations with the Russians should take. Helphand, like Radek, favoured
negotiations in Stockholm. It is likely that the successful Bolshevik
revolution in Russia gave him hope of the possibility of a revolution, or at least a landslide in favour of the Social Democrats, in
Germany.

Haenisch, a friend and admirer of Helphand,[1] summed up Helphand's attitude to war in the following manner: the alliance of Prussian guns and Russian proletariat was the highway to the destruction

of the Tsarist system. But at the same time, the Prussian semi-absolutism, once it was deprived of the protection of the Russian absolutism, would also disappear. Though this analysis of Helphand's views may not have applied before November 1917, it seems to have done after.

Helphand's plan for a Socialist conference in Stockholm was aimed at by-passing the Imperial German government. This, he may have thought, would weaken it and lead to its final overthrow. On the Russian side, this plan was supported by Radek, Hanecki, and Vorovski. (Cf. documents Nos. 100 and 108–11.) These were the men who made a direct attempt at overthrowing the Imperial government, instead of assuming that a revolution in Germany would take place in any case.

This period of Helphand's stay in Stockholm, from the middle of November till the end of December 1917, and the policy he was pursuing there meant the end of Helphand's co-operation with the Foreign Ministry. Though he maintained some contacts with Wilhelmstrasse afterwards, the former degree of their mutual trust was never completely restored. The German government had its way in December 1917; peace between Russia and Germany was negotiated and concluded by the official German government at Brest-Litovsk, the headquarters of the Eastern Command. Helphand had to wait for the defeat of his adopted country and the collapse of the Imperial régime until November 1918.

¹ K. Haenisch, *Parvus*, Berlin, 1925, p. 31.

73

The Imperial Minister in Stockholm to the Foreign Ministry

TELEGRAM NO. 1794

A 37241   8 November 1917, 5.45 p.m.
                                Received: 8 November, 9.45 p.m.

I urgently recommend that all public announcements of amicable agreement with Russia be avoided in the German and Austrian press. Amicable agreement with imperial states cannot possibly be accepted as a watchword by the Bolsheviks. They can only justify peace with Germany by citing the will of the people and Russia's desperate position. Moreover, I am assured from all sides that, in view of their present position, the Russians would only be able to explain friendly words from Germany [*two words garbled*] the weakness of our position in face of the English. It would be advisable for the press to exercise moderation, especially as the extent of the Bolsheviks' victory is not yet certain, since they control the Telegraph Agency.   Lucius

7 4

The State Secretary to the Foreign Ministry Liaison Officer at General Headquarters

TELEGRAM NO. 1748

A 37241   Berlin, 9 November 1917

The view that the utmost moderation should be exercised is shared here.[1] The press has been instructed accordingly. In view of the reports received, it would also be inadvisable for us to make any offers of peace at the front. In the event of offers of a general kind being made by the enemy, these should merely be accepted and no more.

According to further reports from Stockholm, the Bolsheviks there have said that the new government could only remain in power if it achieved a cease-fire in the immediate future. Should an offer to this effect be made at the front, I would ask that I be informed; the High Command of the Army would, of course, immediately be informed of any offer made through other channels. I suggest that any negotiations for a cease-fire by the army should be made with the co-operation of a representative of the Foreign Ministry, and, similarly, that any preliminary discussions or negotiations for peace by the Foreign Ministry be made only with the co-operation of military representatives. Please state whether this proposal is agreed.   Kühlmann

---

[1] i.e. as far as pronouncements concerning a friendly understanding with Russia was concerned.

75

The State Secretary of the Foreign Ministry to the State Secretary of the Treasury

AS 4181   Berlin, 9 November 1917

On the basis of the discussions between Minister von Bergen and Ministerial Director Schröder, I have the honour to request Your Excellency to put the sum of 15 million marks at the disposal of the Foreign Ministry, for use on political propaganda in Russia, charging it to Paragraph 6, Section II of the extraordinary budget. Depending on how events develop, I should like to reserve the possibility of approaching Your Excellency again in the near future with the request that you agree further sums. I should be grateful for a reply as soon as possible.[1]

KÜHLMANN

[1] The sum of 15 million marks was agreed to by the State Secretary of the Treasury on 10 November 1917 (AS 4209 in WK 11c secr, volume 23).

76

The Liaison Officer at General Headquarters to the Foreign Ministry

TELEGRAM NO. 1628

A 37368   9 November 1917, 8.00 p.m.
                          Received: 9 November, 8.30 p.m.

General Ludendorff has sent the following telegram to Eastern Command and to Generals von Mackensen, von Seeckt, and von Cramon (for General von Arz).

'According to intercepted radio transmissions, a revolution has broken out in Petrograd in which the Workers' and Soldiers' Council is supposed to have been victorious. The Council seems to be trying to prevent the withdrawal of troops from the front to Petrograd. The victory of the Workers' and Soldiers' Council is nevertheless desirable from our point of view. I therefore request that you exploit the intercepted radio transmission for propaganda to this end.'

LERSNER

77

The Austro-Hungarian Foreign Minister to the Chancellor

AS 4240   Vienna, 10 November 1917

Your Excellency,

The revolution in Petrograd, which has at least temporarily placed the power into the hands of Lenin and his followers, has come sooner than we had thought possible. Whether or not the Maximalists will be in a position to establish themselves and to exercise governmental power for any length of time, even on the scale on which this was done under Kerenski, will emerge in the next few days. However, numerous signs seem to me to indicate that this question will be answered in the affirmative.

If Lenin and the Bolsheviks should succeed in maintaining their power, then they will be forced to carry out with the utmost vigour the governmental programme which they have formulated. In this context, their promise to bring Russia a 'democratic peace' will occupy first place, and we therefore seem to have reached a decisive turning-point in the peace question.

As I am considerably the younger of the two of us, I am far from wishing to take the initiative or to offer suggestions to Your Excellency, who has much greater experience on which to draw. However, as, after our many discussions about the ramifications of the peace question, I must presume that Your Excellency will also be considering how the altered situation in Russia can best be used to further our aims, I consider it my duty to expound to Your Excellency in this letter the view that I have formed of the situation at this moment, and to present the conclusions that seem to me to arise from it.

Whether or not Lenin and his colleagues will have the power to maintain their supremacy *for any considerable time* is probably a question which nobody can answer. For this very reason, however, it would seem essential to exploit this moment, and to offer them all the help that they would need to produce *faits accomplis* in the peace question. If the Leninists were to succeed even in bringing about the promised armistice, then, it seems to me, we should have won almost a complete victory on the Russian sector, for, if it achieved an armistice, the Russian army, in its present state, would surely pour back into the hinterland in order to be on the spot when the estates are distributed.

In the present circumstances, an armistice would make this army vanish, not to reappear at the front within the forseeable future.

From what I know of Lenin's ideas and intentions, they are directed first of all towards renewing the attempt to achieve *general peace*, and next, if the Western powers would not permit the former, towards concluding a separate peace with us. According to reports received from Petrograd, Lenin has already approached the Western Powers with a view to obtaining their agreement to the conclusion of a general peace, and, according to my information, has given them only a short time in which to answer his request. If, as we can presume with reasonable certainty, the other Entente Powers refuse, then Lenin will be faced with the decision to turn his idea of a separate peace with the Central Powers into a reality. However, he will only wish to do this, or be able to, if we accept the formula, peace 'without annexations or reparations'.

We should certainly be furthering this course of development if we were once again to announce to the men in power in Russia in some sufficiently friendly way that we still adhere to the principles for peace which we have formulated, that is, those set out in the peace resolution passed in the Reichstag, in Herr von Kühlmann's speech, in my various announcements, and in our answers to the Pope's peace note. On the basis of such declarations by the Central Powers, and after the rejection of a general peace without annexations or reparations by the Western Powers, Lenin could then easily make advances towards a separate peace with us within the terms of his programme, and could proceed to the conclusion of an armistice. Since the Maximalists' programme includes the concession of the right to self-determination of the non-Russian peoples of Russia, the question of what should finally be done with Congress Poland, Courland, Livonia, and Finland could well be left to be decided in the course of peace negotiations. It would be our business to ensure that the desire for separation from Russia and for political and economic dependence on the Central Powers be voiced from within these nations. In view of what I have said, I therefore believe that we could influence the development of the situation in Russia favourably to our aims, if, as soon as possible, we were to make declarations to the effect stated and such as would be sufficient to enable the Maximalists to enter into direct negotiations with us without any fears. As far as I am concerned, I would consider allowing myself to be interviewed, for the reports received from Petrograd offer sufficient grounds for a comprehensive answer.

In view of our great military successes on the Italian front, there is now no reason to fear that a statement in these terms could be interpreted as a sign of our weakness: nor can I see that any other harmful effects could result from such a step. In addition, a further advantage which we should gain from this step is that we should take every gust of wind out of the sails of our Socialist parties, with whom Lenin is already trying to open relations. Lenin's desire to negotiate with the Socialist parties of the Central Powers about peace is, in the last analysis, only an attempt to kindle the social revolution in the states of the Central Powers, as a defence for Russia in place of his now almost useless military apparatus. However, if we, as governments, take up the basic standpoint of peace without annexations or reparations, then the ground will be removed from under the feet of this new Socialist conference before it assembles; and it seems to me important that we should make such a meeting superfluous.

I should be most obliged to Your Excellency if you would be good enough to examine the ideas which I have developed here, and to give me your opinion of the matter as soon as possible. In my opinion, we should not allow this moment to pass unexploited, nor miss any opportunity of bringing the war in the East to an end. For the second time, we are being offered the chance of achieving this end by quick action. I doubt whether the possibility will arise again in such favourable circumstances. I need not enumerate the opportunities, both military and political, which will be offered to us, and especially to Germany, if we can finish with the Russians now. I would, on the other hand, like to emphasize the economic factor, for, after a break with the Western Powers, Russia will be forced to rely economically on the Central Powers, who will then have the opportunity of penetrating and reorganizing Russian economic life. The significance of this for the future needs no further comment.

Yours, &c.,
CZERNIN

P.S. Since I ended this letter, a telegram has arrived from Petrograd, containing the basic principles for an offer of peace, decided on by the Soviet Congress, and these confirm the accuracy of the idea, which I expressed above, that Lenin's group is determined to put its peace programme into effect as quickly as possible and that it is, for the moment, still proposing a general peace. However, it must be clear to the Maximalists that a general peace cannot develop from their suggestions, since their ideas are by nature directed more against the Western Powers than against us. I therefore think that the premises underlying my suggestions have been reinforced by the offer of peace made by the Soviet Congress.[1]

[1] This letter was one of two enclosures sent by Hertling, the Imperial Chancellor, to Kühlmann on 12 November. Hertling was in Munich at the time and Czernin's letter was handed over to him by Thun, the Austro-Hungarian Minister there. Hertling expressed his agreement in principle with Czernin's arguments, but reserved the right to define his attitude more precisely later. He asked Kühlmann what proposals he had to make.

78

The Under State Secretary to the Minister in Stockholm

TELEGRAM NO. 1526

AS 4178   Berlin, 10 November 1917

In answer to Telegram No. 1796.[1]

For Riezler.

Half of desired sum will be taken on Sunday by Feldjäger. Remainder on Tuesday. Further sums available if necessary. If more war loan is to be sent, please inform me whether in large or small denominations. Send acknowledgement of receipt to Bergen.

BUSSCHE

[1] See document No. 72.

79

The Counsellor of Legation in Copenhagen to the Foreign Ministry

TELEGRAM NO. 1329

AS 4211   10 November 1917
Dispatched: 11 November, 12.30 a.m.
Received: 11 November, 5.10 a.m.

In continuation of telegram No. 812 of 3 November.[1]

L[öwenstein],[2] who has so far received 2,000 kronen, i.e. 5,000 marks, urgently requests further 20,000 marks. The majority of the sum is needed for the journey of two confidential agents to Petrograd. The journey is necessary, as written communications with Z[ivin] are uncertain nowadays.[3] It appears essential to speed up the matter, as longer inactivity may arouse suspicion. Please telegraph instructions.

L[öwenstein] further asked me to report his appreciation of the situation, also for the information of Bern: 'Lenin needs German support to carry out his programme. This means that the German Government must publicly recognize the war aims of the majority parties. Since these war aims more or less coincide with those of the Bolsheviks, Lenin can ask the Allies to open negotiations on this basis; if they decline to do so Russia will be free of any obligations to the Entente. If the conditions made by the Central Powers are more difficult than those contained in the declaration of the majority parties, they will frustrate Lenin's intention of concluding peace. This would be followed by either his turning to the right or by another revolution. The reports of the proposed separation of Poland and Lithuania from Russia have, at the present moment, weakened confidence in German policy; a reassuring declaration would be valuable.'

L[öwenstein] would be thankful for information as to how to handle the above-mentioned problems and to instruct the agents who will go to Russia.   WITTGENSTEIN

[1] AS 4092 in WK 2 secr, volume 51. A telegram which recommended the plans of Zivin.
[2] Löwenstein, a friend of Zivin, the Social Revolutionary, whom Zivin had introduced to the German Minister in Bern.
[3] Romberg reported on 23 October 1917 (AS 4023 in WK 2 secr, volume 51) a rumour circulating in Russian circles in Switzerland that Zivin had been imprisoned on a charge of high treason. The provisional government appeared to have had proofs that Zivin had some connexions with the Central Powers.

80

The Under State Secretary to the Minister in Copenhagen

TELEGRAM NO. 840

11 November 1917

In reply to telegram No. 1329.

20,000 marks for Blau[1] approved. He can send a message to Russia that the Imperial government still stands on the basis of

the Reichstag resolution. If necessary this can be stressed publicly when the opportunity arises.

BUSSCHE

¹ Löwenstein's cover name.

81

The Counsellor of Legation in Stockholm to the Chancellor

REPORT NO. 1413

A 38075   12 November 1917

The news of their friends' victory is believed to have put the
Bolsheviks here into a state of high excitement and even to have
robbed them of their sleep. They seem to think that they will
soon be the ambassadors of the new Russia, and pretend to be
well informed about the smallest details. However, they have
not as yet actually received any instructions from Petrograd.

At the moment I do not think that the new government in
Petrograd, supposing that it should succeed in securing its power
sufficiently and in maintaining it for at least a few weeks, will
employ Radek, Fürstenberg, and Vorovski¹ as intermediaries.
No clear picture can be gained of the relationship between the
Bolshevik representatives here and the leaders in Petrograd.
Since the presence of the actual leaders of the Petrograd movement, Lenin, Zinoviev, and Trotsky, must be required on the
spot, where unparalleled confusion demands the exercise of their
full authority at every moment, it is nevertheless possible that
the Bolsheviks, should they be able to form a government at all,
may give important commissions to their representatives here.

The most energetic and most talented of these is the Pole
Sobelsohn, well known to German Social Democrats from his
German past, who usually goes under the pseudonym Karl
Radek. As a student, he is supposed to have stolen books and
other such things and therefore to have been given the nickname
Kradek (thief) by his friends. The Russian newspapers still
speak of him under this name, and he has proudly formed his
pseudonym from it. He is described as being quite unscrupulous,
but very clever and extremely talented as an author; and it is
said that, in spite of all his ideological principles, he is not deaf
to opportunist considerations. For the moment his industrious-
ness and his knowledge of German politics—he is well informed

even about secret events—should assure respect in Petrograd for his ideas and suggestions.

Of the leaders in Petrograd, Lenin and Trotsky are supposed to be the most important. Both spent formative years in the West; both far surpass their Social Patriotic opponents in strength of personality, and both are practical revolutionaries in the grand manner. Lenin, a Tartar by the name of Ulyanov, and apparently the organizer and leader of this well-run and circumspectly led movement, is a theorist as regards radical ends, but is practical and direct in the use of means. Trotsky, whose real name is Braunstein, was in France until the outbreak of the war, but was hounded out of that country, supposedly because of his knowledge of Izvolski's guilt in the murder of Jaurés. From Switzerland he fled to Spain, and from there, with the help of the Spanish Socialists, to America. On his return, after the outbreak of the revolution, he was forcibly taken off his ship by the English and put in prison, and he is said to have brought a burning hatred of the English back with him from this journey. If, in spite of the opposition of the whole administration, those now in power should succeed in forming a proper government, he is held up as the most probable Foreign Minister.

Both Lenin and Trotsky are supposed to have enormous personal authority amongst their followers. They are probably capable of keeping order in their party, and of securing and maintaining dictatorial power. In contrast to the Mensheviks, the Bolshevik theorists had jettisoned the parliamentary theory as early as 1906, setting up the idea of the revolutionary dictatorship of a small committee of determined leaders as their only possible course. If, therefore, the new government comes into existence at all and succeeds in breaking down the opposition of the entire bourgeois world, it will not have to defend its own position and its freedom of action, in speeches and assemblies and even against its own followers, to the same extent as its predecessors.

Even if the power of the Bolsheviks in Russia only lasts a few weeks, the country will almost certainly have to face terror such as even France under Marat hardly experienced. The Bolsheviks attacked the Social Revolutionary party for trying to prevent the peasants from burning down farms and seizing land by force. Once in possession of power, which they hope to preserve by making use of the peasants' hunger for land, they will be incapable of stopping the incendiarism which they were defending only a little while before. The peasants will seize by force the land that has been promised them and the soldiers will hurry home from the trenches so as not to come off second-best. Should they capture Kerensky, Miliukov, and Tereschenko, who let the peace and land questions 'rot to stinking corpses', then these men can be sure of a quick and energetically run trial. The Bolsheviks will presumably try to put the entire executive into the hands of the local Workers' and Soldiers' Councils and completely to eliminate the existing administrative machinery. If they are successful in this, even for only a few weeks and even if no cease-fire agreement should be reached, the country will cease to figure in military and economic calculations concerning the World War, and it would take the old régime, which would presumably be restored in this case, years to restore order among the chaos.

Should the present civil war, which is still undecided, end in the defeat of the Bolsheviks, then their watchword 'Peace and Land', once thrown to the masses, will continue to have enormous effects and will force any new government that does not sooner or later want to face another Bolshevik rising, at least to make a pretence of following in the footsteps of the Bolsheviks on these two issues.

RIEZLER

[1] The name Vorovski is spelled Orlowski in the German original.

82

The State Secretary to the Minister in Munich

TELEGRAM NO. 102

AS 4240   Berlin, 13 November 1917

For the Imperial Chancellor.

I humbly thank Your Excellency for your letter of yesterday's date and for the enclosures accompanying it.[1]

As Your Excellency already knows, on 9 November the Petrograd Telegraph Agency published the conditions which had been accepted by the Congress of Workers' and Soldiers' Councils for an offer of peace. This announcement was published in our press on Monday, after the High Command of the Army had dropped their original objections to its publication.

As early as Saturday, Count Czernin had urgently recommended that the Russian announcement should be the subject of favourable discussion, couched in similar terms to those used in the commentary which he had published in his foreign bulletin, in our semi-official organs. In answer to this, I raised the objection that, judging by all the reports received so far, the struggle for power between Lenin and Kerensky was not yet over, that the Bolshevik régime could by no means be regarded as stable, and that by prematurely taking up the unofficial Bolshevik announcement, the terms of which had only been reported here by the Telegraph Agency, we should only be taking the risk of appearing weak.

I am still not prepared to drop this objection. I have just received the following private report (not yet confirmed) from Stockholm: 'According to authentic reports just received, Kerensky, together with Kornilov and Kaledin, has occupied Petrograd. Lenin and his followers have entrenched themselves in the Smolny quarter. Informed Russian circles here believe that the Bolshevik rising has, for the moment, been liquidated, and that any future government in Russia has no choice but to follow a determined peace policy.' According to reports from our Legation in Stockholm, the Entente Powers are reckoning with the collapse of the Bolshevik government within two to three weeks. The refusal of the Russian Legation in Copenhagen to recognize the present government is symptomatic of this conviction. In these circumstances, I think that it would be wiser first of all to await the further course of events in Petrograd. Should the Bolsheviks really succeed in keeping their government in power, we would still be in a position to take up a Russian offer of peace or of an armistice at any moment, and to exploit the opportunities enumerated by Count Czernin better than we could at the present time. A nervous and hasty policy in this matter would only spoil things, and would, in addition, be condemned by German public opinion.

KÜHLMANN

¹ See document No. 77.

83

The Minister in Bern to the Foreign Ministry

TELEGRAM NO. 1833

AS 4279   15 November 1917
Dispatched: 16 November, 1 a.m.
Received: 16 November, 4.55 a.m.

For Bergen. Baier asked that Nasse[1] should be told of the following telegram from Stockholm: 'Please fulfill your promise immediately. We have committed ourselves on this basis,[2] because
great demands are being made on us. Vorovski.' Baier let me
know that this message may make his journey to the North more
urgent.
                                                    ROMBERG

[1] Nasse was in Berlin at the time.
[2] Vorovski was probably alluding to the conclusion of peace between Russia
and Germany.

84

The Under State Secretary to the Foreign Ministry Liaison Officer at General Headquarters

TELEGRAM NO. 1804

A 38241   Berlin, 16 November 1917

Christo Rakovsky, a Rumanian Socialist born in Bulgaria, runs
a Russian socialist paper in Stockholm. Formerly, he was connected with us and he was working for us in Rumania.[1] Rakovsky
asked whether his wife, at present in Bucharest, could be allowed
to come to him in Stockholm. This request, supported by the
Bulgarian Minister, is approved here.
                                                    BUSSCHE

[1] In 1915 Bussche was the German Minister in Bucharest. Rakovsky spent most
of his time there as well, leading the Rumanian Socialist party and editing its daily
newspaper. On 13 January 1915 Bussche telegraphed to the Foreign Ministry (telegram No. 49, AS 161 in Deutschland Nr. 128, Nr. 2 secr, volume 20): 'The Rumanian Socialists, whose leader, Rakovsky, has close connexions with the Italian
Socialists, want to resume, in the press and at public meetings, keen agitation
against Rumania's entry into the war against the Central Powers. I am in a position
to let them have money in an inconspicuous manner, which Südekum was not successful in doing. I regard the matter as important and I beg you to approve the
expenditure of 100,000 Lei for this purpose. I have to have the reply before Friday
morning. Bussche.' The day after, the Deputy State Secretary telegraphed his
approval to Bucharest.
      Helphand was there at the time, on his way from Constantinople to Vienna. It

is very likely that he acted as intermediary between Bussche and Rakovsky. On 14 January Bussche wrote to Zimmermann, enclosing a number of reports, among them one from Helphand, who wrote: 'Apart from Batsaria I talked to Christo Rakovsky, whose energetic stand for peace is well known. He is also of the opinion that it can be expected that Rumania will declare war on the Central Powers shortly' (AS 209 in Deutschland Nr. 128, Nr. 2 secr, volume 20).

Later on in the year Bussche reported from Bucharest that a Socialist demonstration for peace, with Rakovsky as the main speaker, took place on 4 July. Bussche made it clear in his report that the 'demonstration was supported by me and the Austro-Hungarian Ministry' (A 20932 in Deutschland Nr. 128, Nr. 2 secr, volume 35). At the end of 1916, after Rumania had entered the war on the side of the Allies, Rakovsky was arrested by the Rumanian authorities for conducting propaganda against the war.

It is interesting to note in this connexion that a reference was made, at the Moscow trials, to Rakovsky's activities in Rumania in 1915. (*Report of Court Proceedings in the case of the Anti-Soviet 'Block of Rights and Trotskyites'*, Moscow, 1938, pp. 300–1.) In 1924 one Armstrong allegedly used a letter, dating from 1915, to blackmail Rakovsky into joining the British intelligence service. The following conversation between Vishinsky and Rakovsky is the verbatim report of the relevant part of the trial:

Vishinsky: For whom was this letter intended?

Rakovsky: This letter was written to Germany, but there was no address.

V.: The letter was intended for Germany?

R.: It followed from the content that it was intended for the German government.

V.: For the German intelligence service?

R.: Possibly.

V.: What did the letter say?

R.: The letter said approximately the following: I am enclosing a list of Rumanian commercial firms and newspaper offices which should be won over to the side of Germany in order to draw Rumania itself into the war on the side of Germany.

V.: What was the meaning of these contents of the letter?

R.: The contents of the letter meant that there existed a connexion between me and the German intelligence service, the German government, or some German organization.

V.: And you helped Germany in enlisting Rumanian citizens on Rumanian territory to aid Germany?

R.: Yes.

There are, in the Rumanian files of the German Foreign Ministry, lists of firms and newspapers which it was intended to bring under German influence. They came from Roselius, a Bremen merchant active in the Balkans at the time. None of them bears Rakovsky's signature. How Rakovsky or Vishinsky knew about their existence is a mystery.

85

The Minister in Stockholm to the Foreign Ministry

TELEGRAM NO. 1854

AS 4337

19 November 1917, 3.50 p.m.
Received: 19 November, 7.20 p.m.

Parvus has received urgent call from Adolf Müller to come to Switzerland, presumably for negotiations with Italian Socialists.

He has refused. He suggests that Müller be informed that he has opened contacts with Petrograd and sees prospects of negotiations in near future. He promises 'the furtherance of [*one word garbled*] with regard to Russia'. Riezler.

Lucius

86

The Legation in Stockholm to the Foreign Ministry

TELEGRAM NO. 1870

AS 4368   22 November 1917, 3.05 p.m.
                                Received: 22 November, 7.50 p.m.

For Deputy Erzberger and Counsellor Nadolny.

Parvus's undertaking has come to knowledge of Russian colony here prematurely and has been viewed unfavourably. Even circles close to the Bolsheviks have raised objections to his being entrusted with such a delicate mission, saying that German Social Democrats would present Bolshevik's opponents with a powerful weapon by 'electing' a man like him as courier, while the other side says that hardly are the Bolsheviks at the helm before Parvus pays them their allowance. It is believed that Parvus's appearance in Petrograd will endanger the imminently expected formation of a Democratic coalition there.

Immediately on my arrival yesterday, I had detailed discussion, in the terms set out in the memorandum which I gave to Herr Erzberger on Sunday, with our people who, in turn, made contact with the Bolshevik leader Vorovski. According to Russian press, Vorovski has been appointed representative, and he is expecting official confirmation at any moment. Meanwhile, some Bolsheviks have asked police here what they would do if Bolsheviks arrested Russian Minister here, who refuses to vacate his position. Police naturally declined to answer. Typical of Bolsheviks.

Wucherpfennig
Legation

8 7

The Minister in Bern to the Foreign Ministry

TELEGRAM NO. 1862

A 39102   22 November 1917
Dispatched: 23 November, 2 a.m.
Received: 23 November, 4 a.m.

A reliable, extremely well-informed agent reports the following in strictest confidence: 'The planned transport of *emigrés* includes all the Bolsheviks and Internationalists who were left behind in Switzerland by the previous transports, among them whole families with wives and children. The Internationalists are the left wing of the Mensheviks, who were represented by Martov at Zimmerwald and who are fighting for the development and strengthening of "the Russian revolution on the basis of a class-conscious independence of the proletariat". One of them is Bagocki, the President of the Russian Committee of Emigrés in Zürich. Bagocki is a Pole, educated in Russia; he will stay in Petrograd. Another of those to travel is Dr. Kornblum, a friend of Lenin and a leading politician, who stayed behind in order to take a degree in chemistry.

'According to the decision of the Central Committee, only the "illegals", i.e. the genuine *emigrés* who are active in the revolution will be transported to Russia: this time no exception should be made for those *emigrés* who may have sympathized with the "illegals".

'The *emigrés* can leave seven days after permission to travel is granted.

'They have done nothing about their Swedish entry or transit visas because they do not know whether this is necessary or desirable.'

Deputy Adolf Müller urgently supports this application and recommends us to grant permission to travel as soon as possible. Panov has not yet come to see me.   ROMBERG

88

The Under State Secretary to the Foreign Ministry Liaison Officer at General Headquarters

TELEGRAM NO. 783

A 38976   Berlin, 25 November 1917

The committee of the Russian *emigrés* in Zürich has applied, through the intermediary of Chief Justice Zgraggen, for permission for 50 to 100 Russian *emigrés* (including women and children) to travel through Germany under the same conditions as those made for the previous convoys.

Since most of them are probably Bolsheviks, the application is approved by us. For the moment the *emigrés* have been told that they must first of all procure Swedish entry visas. According to a report from the Imperial Legation in Stockholm, the Swedish Minister in Petrograd has telegraphed, saying that, in view of the state of the railways, returning *emigrés* should not be sent on to the frontier. In order to avoid the massing of returning *emigrés* in its country the Swedish government has therefore stopped the issue of entry visas.

I would ask Your Excellency to find out from the High Command of the Army whether the *emigrés* journey may take place in the event of their procuring Swedish visas. If so, the Political Section would have to be instructed accordingly.[1]

BUSSCHE

[1] Reply from Lersner: A 40476 in WK 2 secr, volume 53: Report No. 1040, 1.12.17. 'There are no objections in the General Headquarters to the transport of the emigrants if they acquire Swedish visas. The Political Section, Berlin will be informed. Lersner.'

89

The Counsellor of Legation in Stockholm to the Chancellor

REPORT NO. 1484

A 39974   Stockholm, 26 November 1917

Subject: The situation in Petrograd.

One's joy at the courage and determination of the Bolshevik government must not lead one to put too much faith in the

optimistic claims for the duration of their government being
made by the Bolsheviks here. For example, since Lenin's victory,
the representatives here have asserted every day that the efforts
to form a coalition with the other Socialist parties would unquestionably be successful in the very near future, and that this
would secure the existence of the new government and ensure
its ability to act. So far these efforts have not only been unsuccessful, but the very question of forming a coalition has led
to violent differences amongst the Bolsheviks themselves and to
the separation of a considerable number of their followers. To
illustrate the uncertain attitude of the Bolshevik government,
I would draw your attention to the telegram of the 23rd from
the Haparanda press office. For the moment, we are dealing
with what is simply the forceful dictatorship of a handful of
determined revolutionaries, whose domination is held in complete contempt by the rest of Russia and is only tolerated because these men promise immediate peace and, as is generally
known, will bring it.

By any reasonable judgement, the supremacy of these people
will shake the whole Russian state to its roots and, in all probability, in not more than a few months, when the *raison
d'être* of the new government has ceased to exist, and the war
against other nations has finally been brought to an end, it will
then be swept away by a flood of violent hostility throughout
the rest of Russia.

It is in the light of this situation that the usefulness of Goldberg's activities, which were set in motion by Deputy Erzberger,
must be judged. However correct the policy of agreement, which
was laid down in the Reichstag on 19 July as a continuation of
Imperial Chancellor von Bethmann-Hollweg's policy, may be,
it must not tempt one to adopt the idea that a *rapprochement* between the German people and the Russian people—in the sense
of friendship between peoples—should be initiated through
negotiations between the majority parties and delegates of those
now in power in Russia. It is this idea that Goldberg has thrust
into the foreground. It would probably be a grave political error
even to seem to bind the future of Russo-German relations to
the fortunes of the men now in power in Russia. The duration
of their government will bring no more than a cease-fire and
possibly a formal peace. In the circumstances, and in view of the
violent shocks which are in all probability still facing Russia,
we shall not be able to take up proper peaceful communications
and a friendly, neighbourly relationship once more until some

considerable time has elapsed and a start is made in the gradual restoration of order. That will be the time to begin working for agreements, with the Russian people and with another Russian government, such as those Goldberg has in mind. Until then, only a cautious handling of commercial issues by representatives of the actual government will be possible or to the point, and only action of this kind will enable us to achieve a transition to good relations, even with a new government and a Russia which is not Bolshevik.

RIEZLER

90

The Minister in Stockholm to the Chancellor

REPORT NO. 1482

A 39975   Stockholm, 26 November 1917

Subject: Deputy Erzberger's discussions with the Bolsheviks.

In the light of my observations in the past, and especially after the discussion I had yesterday with my Bulgarian colleague, who has excellent connexions with Russian Socialists of all shades, I can only subscribe to the report[1] which Your Excellency received from Counsellor Riezler, in which he said that the discussions between Deputy Erzberger and the Bolsheviks here, which have already lasted a considerable time, have created great uncertainty, to the detriment of the general negotiations. With his notorious vanity, Erzberger has been determined to win a personal success and he let the Bolsheviks know, some considerable time ago, that the German people wanted peace and that an agreement with him, Erzberger—as the representative of the majority parties—would also bind the Imperial government.[2] This has undoubtedly created the double misconception in the minds of the Bolsheviks—who are very naïve in political matters—that there is a great hunger for peace in Germany and that there is a split between the representatives of the people and the government, of which the latter can be ignored. Such a belief must, of necessity, not only make Counsellor Riezler's task more difficult, but must also weaken the authority of any declaration made by the government.

Judging by what I have found out about Erzberger's negotiations so far, for example those with Kolyshko, about which Hugo Stinnes, amongst others, is very well informed,[3] I regard him as extremely ill-suited to negotiate with the Russians, to whom he has already made the most dangerous confidences about our internal and external affairs. For example, the discussion lasting several hours which a confidential agent of Deputy Erzberger was instructed to hold with Vorovski, resulted in the latter ironically telling a German, soon afterwards, that the men in Petrograd now knew all about the mood of all the German parties. The Germans, too, needed peace.

LUCIUS

[1] Document No. 89.

[2] Kühlmann's marginal comment: 'An end should be finally put to this.'

[3] According to German sources, Kolyshko was, for fifteen years, the private secretary of Baron Witte. In June 1915 he came to Stockholm with an American called Passwell, who introduced Kolyshko to the German Minister there. Kolyshko expressed his willingness to conduct pro-German peace propaganda in Russia in the Ruskoe Slovo. Rantzau, from Copenhagen, advocated reserve and caution in the treatment of Kolyshko and his plans.

In July 1916 Kolyshko made another appearance in Stockholm, this time accompanied by Prince Bebutov. Bockelmann, an agent of the Foreign Ministry, negotiated with them. It became clear during these negotiations that the two Russians regarded the setting up of a publishing house, which would become the centre of pro-German propaganda, as extremely desirable. Warburg, a member of the Hamburg banking family, thought the project not only plausible, but profitable.

Hugo Stinnes, the industrialist, was also interested in the negotiations between the Russians and Bockelmann, but regarded the whole business, in its initial stages, with animosity. Stinnes wanted to play the leading role, but Lucius, the German Minister in Stockholm, maintained that Bockelmann, who had relations with prominent Russians, was much more suitable to conduct the negotiations than Trenck or Fehrmann, Stinnes's agents in Scandinavia.

On 12 August 1916 a compromise was finally reached between Stinnes and Bockelmann. Stinnes undertook to lend Bockelmann 2 million roubles for the financing of a publishing house in Russia. Two days later Jagow, the State Secretary in the Foreign Ministry, and Stinnes signed an agreement in Berlin, by which the Foreign Ministry reserved the right to control the undertaking as far as the relations between Germany and Russia were concerned.

It is likely that some of the money intended for influencing the Russian press in favour of Germany and peace reached, via Kolyshko, Maxim Gorki's paper *Novaia Zhizn*.

Fehrmann wrote in one of his reports for Stinnes (AS 1800 in WK 2 secr, volume 36): 'It [*Novaia Zhizn*] has started to appear only now [May 1917] and therefore the presumption remains justified that our friend is connected with it. He probably has Gorki work on purely Social Democrat lines, in order to keep the *Lutch* in reserve for himself.'

Before Kolyshko was arrested by the Provisional government in the summer of 1917, he went over to Stockholm once more. He saw Erzberger there on that occasion. The documents on the separate peace negotiations in which Kolyshko, Bebutov, Protopopov, Erzberger, Bockelmann, Warburg, and others took part can be found mainly in the series WK 2 secr, and WK 2. The key documents for the negotiations for the establishment of a publishing house in Russia are in Russland Nr. 74 secr, volume 2. The Nachlass Jagow, the private papers of the one-time State Secretary, also contain some interesting material on these negotiations.

91

The Minister in Bern to the Foreign Ministry

TELEGRAM NO. 1895

AS 4446   26 November 1917
Dispatched: 27 November, 2.30 p.m.
Received: 27 November, 4.10 p.m.

For Bergen. Baier must postpone his departure by a week on medical advice. Nasse is also staying here for the time being. In the meantime, the requested financial aid is being dispatched through safe channels.

ROMBERG

92

The Under State Secretary to the Minister in Bern

TELEGRAM NO. 1367

AS 4446   Berlin, 28 November 1917

In answer to Telegram No. 1895.

According to information received here, the government in Petrograd is having to fight against great financial difficulties. It is therefore very desirable that they be sent money. Bergen.

BUSSCHE

93

The Liaison Officer at General Headquarters to the Foreign Ministry

TELEGRAM NO. 1771

AS 4486   29 November 1917, 7.25 p.m.
Received: 29 November, 7.35 p.m.

For the attention of the State Secretary.

Should there be peace negotiations with Russia in the foreseeable future, His Majesty requests that Your Excellency should, in spite of everything, still try to reach some kind of alliance or friendly relations with the Russians. He said that, as after the Russo-Japanese war, this might be easier than we now thought. He had already won the High Command of the Army over to the idea of getting the Russian railways running, if this were possible, and of putting German Railway General Staff officers at the Russians' disposal for this purpose. In the more distant future, the Emperor also hopes to set up a close commercial relationship with the Russians.[1]

LERSNER

[1] Kühlmann's marginal note: 'For Bergen. Please draft a reply which would not be binding.' (Bitte einen Antwort aber 'ohne obligo'.)

94

The State Secretary to the Foreign Ministry Liaison Officer at General Headquarters

TELEGRAM NO. 1925

AS 4486   Berlin, 3 December 1917

The disruption of the Entente and the subsequent creation of political combinations agreeable to us constitute the most important war aim of our diplomacy. Russia appeared to be the weakest link in the enemy chain. The task therefore was gradually to loosen it, and, when possible, to remove it. This was the purpose of the subversive activity we caused to be carried out in Russia behind the front—in the first place promotion of separatist tendencies and support of the Bolsheviks. It was not until the Bolsheviks had received from us a steady flow of funds through various channels and under different labels that they were in a position to be able to build up their main organ, *Pravda*, to conduct energetic propaganda and appreciably to extend the originally narrow basis of their party. The Bolsheviks have now come to power; how long they will retain power cannot be yet foreseen. They need peace in order to strengthen their own position; on the other hand it is entirely in our interest that we should exploit the period while they are in power, which may be a short one, in order to attain firstly an armistice and then, if possible, peace.[1] The conclusion of a separate peace would mean the achievement of the desired war aim, namely a breach between Russia and her Allies. The amount of tension necessarily caused by such a breach would determine the degree of Russia's dependence on Germany and her future relations with us. Once cast out and cast off by her former Allies, abandoned financially, Russia will be forced to seek our support. We shall be able to provide help for Russia in various ways; firstly in the rehabilitation of the railways; (I have in mind a German Russian Commission, under our control, which would undertake the rational and co-ordinated exploitation of the railway lines so as to ensure speedy resumption of freight movement), then the provision of a substantial loan, which Russia requires to maintain her state machine. This could take the form of an advance on the security of grain, raw materials, &c., &c., to be provided by Russia and shipped under the control of the above-mentioned commission. Aid on such a basis—the scope to be increased as and when necessary—would in my opinion bring about a growing *rapprochement* between the two countries.

Austria-Hungary will regard the *rapprochement* with distrust and not without apprehension. I would interpret the excessive eagerness of Count Czernin to come to terms with the Russians as a desire to forestall us and to prevent Germany and Russia arriving at an intimate relationship inconvenient to the Danube Monarchy. There is no need for us to compete for Russia's good will. We are strong enough to wait with equanimity; we are in a far better position than Austria-Hungary to offer Russia what she needs for the reconstruction of her state. I view future developments in the East with confidence but I think it expedient for the time being to maintain a certain reserve in our attitude to the Austro-Hungarian government in all matters including the Polish question which concern both monarchies so as to preserve a free hand for all eventualities.

The above-mentioned considerations lie, I venture to believe, within the framework of the directives given me by His Majesty. I request you to report to His Majesty accordingly and to transmit to me by telegram the All-highest instructions.

KÜHLMANN

[1] The words 'there can be no question of further support of the Bolsheviks' in Bergen's draft of this telegram were not dispatched. A copy of this telegram, as it was received and decoded at the General Headquarters, is in WK Gr. Hauptquartier Nr. 31b, volume 1. The editor is indebted to Mr. George Katkov, who gave his kind permission to reproduce here his translation of this and the subsequent document. See Mr. Katkov's article in *International Affairs*, volume 32, No. 2.

95

The Liaison Officer at the Imperial Court to the Foreign Ministry

TELEGRAM NO. 1819

AS 4607

4 December 1917, 7.30 p.m.
Received: 4 December 8.25 p.m.

In reply to telegram No. 1925.

His Majesty the Kaiser has expressed his agreement with Your Excellency's *exposé* about a possible *rapprochement* with Russia.

GRÜNAU

96

The Under State Secretary to the Foreign Ministry Liaison Officer at General Headquarters

TELEGRAM NO. 1943

A 40476

Berlin, 5 December 1917

In reply to report No. 1040.[1]

The Swedish government has informed us that visas cannot be given to the Russian *emigrés* until there is a guarantee that they will be allowed entry into Russia.

As this information cannot be obtained through other channels, and as the *emigrés* in question are supposed to be close to Lenin, I request that you ask the High Command of the Army to ask the Russian Government, by radio-telegraph or through the Russians negotiating for a cease-fire, whether it will grant entry to the *emigrés* who wish to return from Switzerland to Russia through Germany and, if so, whether it will inform the Swedish government accordingly. Alternatively, it might be possible to let the *emigrés* through our lines and those of the Russians.

BUSSCHE

[1] See document No. 88, footnote 1.

97

The Under State Secretary to the Political Section of the Deputy General Staff in Berlin

A 40476   5 December 1917

Copy[1] humbly sent to the Political Section of the General Staff in Berlin, with reference to the instructions about the return of Russian *emigrés* from Switzerland sent directly to the Political Section by the High Command of the Army. According to a report from the Imperial Legation in Bern, the Russian author Karl Buchholz, who, according to a letter of 3 September from the Deputy General Staff was refused permission to travel from Switzerland to Sweden through Germany, intends to join up with the *emigrés* in question. Since Buchholz is supposed to be on good terms with Lenin, and since he now wants to travel not to Sweden, but to Russia, it seems advisable to allow him and the other *emigrés* transit through Germany. I would ask for a decision from you in this matter as soon as possible so that the Imperial Legation in Bern can be instructed accordingly.

BUSSCHE

[1] Copy of telegram No. 1943; document No. 96.

98

The Minister in Bern to the Foreign Ministry

TELEGRAM NO. 1949

AS 4636   Bern, 5 December 1917

Dispatched: 6 December, 12.40 a.m.
Received: 5.20 a.m.

For the attention of Herr von Bergen.

Baier sufficiently recovered to travel possibly Saturday, at latest Sunday. I urgently request instructions as to whether journey is desirable.[1] In view of the unusually powerful effect which, as far as can be judged here, has been produced everywhere by the much-publicized interview in the *Freie Presse*,[2] I believe that Baier, with the strong influence which he exercises on the

Bolsheviks, will be in a position actively to counter the hostile exploitation of this interview which was, of course, immediately unleashed with all the means available.   ROMBERG

¹ The reply from the Under Secretary of State: Berlin, 6 December 1917. Telegram No. 1416. 'In answer to telegram No. 1949. Journey desirable. Bergen. BUSSCHE.' (WK 11c secr, volume 23.)
² Goldmann's interview with Hindenburg and Ludendorff, published in the Sunday edition of the *Neue Freie Presse*, 1 December 1917. Ludendorff told Goldmann: 'I do not regard the Bolshevik announcement as an offer of peace . . . We can conclude an armistice with Russia only when we are certain that it will be observed. . . . If somebody were to tell me that the Russian revolution was a lucky chance as far as we were concerned, I would protest: the revolution in Russia was no chance, but the natural and inevitable result of our conduct of the war. . . . It is the outcome of our victory.'

99

Deputy Erzberger to the State Secretary

A 40975   Berlin, 7 December 1917

Your Excellency,

I have the honour to enclose a copy of a report which has just arrived here from Herr Ziese in Stockholm.

Yours, &c.,
ERZBERGER

Enclosure: Stockholm, 5 December 1917

According to the latest reports from Petrograd, Lenin and Trotsky intend severely to punish those Russian Ministers abroad who do not recognize the authority of the Bolshevik government, first of all by stopping all supplies of money. This measure not only affects the accredited Ministers in the Entente countries, but those in neutral states as well.

Gulkevich, the Russian Minister here, has also had his supplies of money stopped. These people are thus in an appalling position. They cannot pay their staff, and nobody will give them credit. An extraordinary situation will now arise, for Lenin and Trotsky will first of all send new Bolshevik representatives to the neutral countries. If these are not recognized, then Trotsky intends not to recognize the Ministers of the countries in question in Petrograd. This would be a great misfortune for us, for it is decidedly to our advantage that the neutral Ministers in

Petrograd should continue in active office, since the Swedish Legation in particular is wholeheartedly and energetically representing German interests there. It would also be of great advantage to us to support the Bolshevik government, as it is definitely working for peace, that is, along the same lines as we. It would therefore be a very good thing if we could persuade the neutral governments to recognize the Bolshevik government and the Bolshevik Ministers in their own countries as quickly as possible. I would ask that this matter in particular be seriously and speedily considered, since it appears to me to be of the utmost importance and since such action would even serve greatly to strengthen the position of the Bolsheviks inside Russia.[1]

The scene inside Russia is an extraordinary one. Quite a number of different, independent republics have been formed. The latest of these, however, are the *German Prisoners' Republics*. In various places where there are large prisoner-of-war camps, the German prisoners, finding that all order had broken down around them, took the business of feeding and administration into their own hands and now feed not only themselves, but also the villages around. The villagers are extremely satisfied with this state of affairs and, together with the prisoners, have formed something like a republican administration, which is directed by the German prisoners. This could surely be called a new phenomenon in the history of the world. Russia, even more than America, is the land of unlimited possibilities.

[1] Kühlmann's marginal remark: 'A copy for His Majesty, without revealing the source, should be seriously considered.' A copy of Ziese's report was sent to Grünau as No. 85 (Russland Nr. 61, volume 137). See also document No. 101.

100

The Minister in Stockholm to the Foreign Ministry

TELEGRAM NO. 1987

A 41289   8 December 1917, 11.55 p.m.
                              Received: 9 December, 2.45 a.m.

Have just had private talk with Vorovski, who gives the impression of being an honest and reasonable man. He thinks that his government is forced by considerations for internal political opponents to leave open the possibility of Allied participation in the negotiations, and could only justify a separate peace by citing the refusal of the Allies to take part. However, he said that appeals to this effect were meant as platonically as calls to peoples to start the revolution. If the appeals were obviously unsuccessful, the Russians would go on to start direct negotiations for a separate peace. The question of peace would probably come up for discussion at the first session of the Constituent Assembly on 11 November, and would probably lead to violent strife with the Kadets. If no methods for negotiation are agreed at the front, he is prepared to suggest a practical method to his government. I explained to him that, in face of the attempts to sabotage or delay the negotiations which we must expect to encounter, only businesslike and practical negotiations between the actual governments can lead to results. He is still toying with the idea of an inter-parliamentary conference, as he would expect such a conference to produce a favourable effect among the Western powers. However, he admits that this method might delay or endanger the outcome. He presumes that his government would prefer the negotiations to take place in a neutral country rather than in the atmosphere of the front. Riezler.

LUCIUS

Note:

Telegraph Lucius immediately,[1] saying that he should tell Vorovski that only Brest can be considered for preliminary peace, as everything is ready there. Choice of a neutral place would greatly lengthen negotiations and would raise countless questions of international etiquette.

Preliminary peace could be concluded in a very short time. Method and place for detailed negotiations, for which I might agree to a neutral meeting-place, would be the subject of direct negotiation. If Trotsky or Lenin came in person, I myself would appear for the negotiations, and this would offer a guarantee of a speedy conclusion. Request Lucius to continue to work energetically along the lines indicated in his telegram of today's date. The inter-parliamentary conference is impossible at the moment and would result in the failure of the efforts being made to achieve peace.

KÜHLMANN

[1] This telegram was dispatched to Stockholm on 10 December 1917 as No. 1684 (WK 2 secr, volume 53).

101

The State Secretary to the Legation in Stockholm

TELEGRAM NO. 1674

A 40975   Berlin, 9 December 1917

The recognition of the Russian Bolshevik government by the official recognition of its diplomatic representatives by neutral states would considerably strengthen the position of the Russian government, which is engaged in negotiations with us. Since, in the event of neutral states refusing to recognize diplomatic representatives appointed by the Bolsheviks, there is a danger that the Russian government might break off relations with the Ministers in Petrograd of the neutral states concerned, and since, moreover, we lay particular value on the continuation of the activities of the Swedish Minister in Petersburg, I request that you discuss the matter confidentially with the Swedish government and recommend them to recognize the Bolshevik representative as soon as possible.

Send report by telegram.

KÜHLMANN

102

The State Secretary to the Legation in Stockholm

TELEGRAM NO. 1675

A 41232   Berlin, 9 December 1917

For Riezler.

Scheidemann left here today to travel to Stockholm via Copenhagen. He apparently intends to try to persuade Bolsheviks to hold peace negotiations with majority Socialists or Reichstag majority. It is our opinion, too, that negotiations must be held only between governments, and preferably at some point at the front. On the other hand, Bolsheviks have already been influenced towards direct negotiations over the head of German government by Goldberg's offer. It is therefore desirable that Scheidemann be persuaded, not only not to strengthen this inclination, but even, as far as possible, to cure them of their idea and to advise them to open negotiations with government quickly. Please therefore seize him immediately on arrival and, before he talks with Bolsheviks, try to convince him of this view, using approximately the following arguments:

1. The Bolsheviks have issued calls to governments and peoples. Moreover, they have already exchanged telegrams and conducted armistice negotiations with the German government and, according to statements in the press, they have expressed satisfaction with these negotiations. They have therefore no reason to by-pass government.

2. Going over the head of the government would be considered unconstitutional here and would not only cause trouble in the government and in the country generally, which might make peace with Russia more difficult to achieve, delay it, or even actually endanger it, but would also lower the reputation of the government in foreign eyes, or at least in the eyes of the Entente. Since government stands by principles of Reichstag resolution and of answer to Pope's peace note,[1] and since peace treaty would anyway only be valid after ratification by Reichstag, there is no reason to distrust or by-pass the latter body either.

Scheidemann would therefore best contribute to quick conclusion of peace by instilling as much confidence in the government as possible into Bolsheviks, and by persuading them to open negotiations soon.

Please therefore draw his attention to the fact that departure from normal channels, or delay, would result in danger of conference with minority Social Democrats, which some people are apparently trying to organize, actually taking place.

Legation in Copenhagen[2] has been instructed to find out day of his arrival in Stockholm and inform you by telegram. Ledebour and Kautzky,[3] who also wanted to travel to Stockholm, are being kept here, and Goldberg and Wucherpfennig are also staying here for the moment. Report by telegram.

KÜHLMANN

---

[1] The Reichstag resolution of the majority parties is discussed in Erzberger, op. cit., pp. 265–9, and the Pope's peace note, pp. 269–87. For the Reichstag resolution cf. Scheidemann, op. cit., volume 2, pp. 359–69.

[2] The Legation in Copenhagen was sent the same telegram under No. 933, with the request to inform the Legation in Stockholm of Scheidemann's arrival (WK 2 secr, volume 53).

[3] Scheidemann was a member of the majority Social Democrat Party, Kautzky and Ledebour led the Socialist faction, the Independent Social Democrat Party.

103

The Minister in Stockholm to the Foreign Ministry

TELEGRAM NO. 2011

A 41669   12 December 1917, 1.45 p.m.
                                    Received: 12 December, 7.52 p.m.

In reply to telegram No. 1684.[1]

Commission completed. Vorovski passed the message immediately to Petrograd, but as he has not yet received any code,
the time of the arrival of his reports is uncertain, if reply [*one
group garbled*] arrives I recommend therefore the same treatment
at armistice negotiations. Riezler.

                                                         Lucius

[1] See document No. 100, footnote 1.

104

*The Under State Secretary to the Liaison Officer at the
Imperial Court*

TELEGRAM NO. 1986

A 41553   Berlin, 13 December 1917

In answer to instructions from this office to recommend to the
Swedish government that it recognize the representative of the
Bolsheviks and thus strengthen the Bolshevik government,[1]
the Imperial Minister in Stockholm telegraphed as follows
on 11 December:[2]

'The Minister of Foreign Affairs is quite prepared to receive
Vorovski and to discuss current business with him. I have let
the latter know this. The Minister said that recognition had
really already been made to the Bolshevik government in
Petrograd by General Brandstroem, in that the Minister there
had courteously acknowledged the Russian note and was
actually conducting current business with the government
through Legation officials. A formal recognition of the new
Russian Minister in Stockholm, who, even in today's interview
with *Dagens Nyheter*, merely described himself as "the Commissar

of the Bolshevik government", could hardly be made until the Constituent Assembly had confirmed the position of the present government.'

The Minister entirely shared Your Excellency's view that the government's position would be strengthened by recognition, and he finally seemed quite prepared to recognize Vorovski as Minister.   BUSSCHE

---

[1] Document No. 101.
[2] A 41553 in Russland Nr. 61, volume 137. Telegram No. 2000.

105

The Deputy State Secretary to the Minister in Stockholm

TELEGRAM NO. 1717

A 41678   Berlin, 13 December 1917

In answer to telegram No. 2011.[1]

For Riezler. Minister in Copenhagen reports[2] that he has heard from a reliable source that Vorovski has written to his confidential agent in Copenhagen, saying that it was desirable that the negotiations should be moved from the front on to neutral territory (possibly Stockholm). To justify this, Vorovski had stated that from neutral territory it would be easier to induce the Entente countries to participate in the negotiations and thus to create a bridge from separate negotiations to general ones. Vorovski had also said that Lenin and Trotsky wanted the negotiations to be conducted by parliamentarians, as this would eliminate the pressures exerted by the armies.

I repeat that, from our point of view, negotiations for a preliminary peace on neutral territory are most undesirable and should be avoided if at all possible. The same goes for an interparliamentary conference. According to reports received here from our representative at Eastern Command (Oberost), the Russian delegates also prefer a place at the front for negotiations, and have not expressed any wish to have parliamentarians taking part.   BUSSCHE

---

[1] Document No. 103.
[2] Telegram No. 1450 of 12 December 1917 (A 41678 in WK 2 secr, volume 53).

106

The Minister in Stockholm to the Foreign Ministry

TELEGRAM NO. 2036

A 42010

15 December 1917, 12.30 a.m.
Received: 15 December, 11.35 a.m.

In answer to telegram No. 1717.

It is true that Vorovski would like negotiations held in Stockholm, and also that he has told friends that the differences between the Reichstag and the Army Command should be exploited. Parvus, who wants to play his part, is also working for the choice of Stockholm. I have made the most strenuous efforts to counter both plans. Vorovski assures me that he has informed Trotsky of my objections. In a discussion lasting several hours, I have just explained to Vorovski in forceful terms that Stockholm would be a most unsuitable choice, and why. In addition, I warned him emphatically against trying any experiments with internal German affairs, telling him that no German party would countenance any such experiment in face of official opinion. I said that the opponents of the Bolsheviks were pressing the German government not to conclude peace with them, as their successors would also have to make peace, but rather to uproot the Bolsheviks in Russia by declaring them incompetent to conduct negotiations. The German government rejected these suggestions, but it could not expose itself to the risk of conducting negotiations under virtually hopeless conditions. Vorovski admitted that a German refusal might cause the fall of the Bolsheviks and only requested that consideration should be given in Berlin to the fact that the Bolsheviks were obliged to stage the negotiations under democratic forms of control and to assure the possibility of immediate publication of results, and that, in addition, they must leave open the possibility of Allied participation. No attempt would be made to influence the composition of the German delegation. After repeated questions, he admitted that he had no detailed instructions from Petrograd as to the views of the men there regarding the form the negotiations should adopt and the course they should take. It seems clear to me that his wishes express the feelings of Parvus and Goldberg rather than those of his government, and that, if no other way is possible, Trotsky in particular will agree to negotiate in Brest, as long as at least the external features of Bolshevik negotiating methods, which are imperative for him too, are preserved. Vorovski admitted that my arguments were justified, even though he will not entirely rid himself of Goldberg's idea of broad negotiations between peoples, which he thinks would result in more acceptable demands. He is sending another report to Petrograd and a direct courier is also on his way there with a serious and forthright report for Trotsky. Riezler.

Lucius

107

The Liaison Officer at General Headquarters to the Foreign Ministry

TELEGRAM NO. 1895

AS 4897   16 December, 1917, 9.15 a.m.
                               Received: 16 December, 9.50 a.m.

The matter[1] is settled, in so far as, following the sessions of 6 and 7 December in Berlin, General Ludendorff has given Eastern Command the following principles for peace discussions:

'1. No interference in Russian affairs.

'2. No war reparations in money, but only financial compensation for the maintenance of prisoners of war, whose total far exceeds 1 million. German annexation of Lithuania and Courland (including Riga and the islands), since we need more land in order to feed the nation. We intend to respect the nationalist demands of the Lithuanians and the Courlanders to a considerable extent in the terms of the annexation. This is conditional on the English not occupying the Aaland Isles, Finland, Estonia, or Livonia.

'3. Exchange of prisoners of war, while recognizing that their work is essential to Germany until general peace. Exchange of civilian prisoners.

'4. Polish independence and the association of Poland with the Central Powers. Settlement of the eastern frontiers of Poland, including the return of the occupied territories to Russia.

'5. Recognition of the right of peoples to self-determination. Russian evacuation of Finland, Estonia, Livonia, the Moldava, Eastern Galicia, and Armenia.

'6. The offer of our good services in the settlement of the question of the Dardanelles and of other problems outside Europe.

'7. Reorganization of the Russian system of communications with German help. Financial support for Russian reconstruction and close economic relations. Settlement of commercial relations. Delivery of cereals, oil, &c., to Germany at favourable prices.

'8. The legal rights of the nationals of either party in the territory of the other shall be restored. Losses of private property, where those suffering were not responsible, shall be made good.

'9. In case the Russian representatives should express a fear of Japanese intervention against Russia, a guarantee that Germany will not attack Russia from behind if she has to defend herself against Japan.

'10. We are prepared to enter into an alliance with Russia at a later date.'

LERSNER

---

[1] i.e. agreement between the military and the Foreign Ministry on preliminary conditions for peace negotiations between Germany and Russia.

108

The Under State Secretary to the Minister in Copenhagen

TELEGRAM NO. 956

AS 4929   Berlin, 17 December 1917

Parvus should come here as soon as possible and on his way here he should call on Your Excellency.[1] Please ask him urgently to help to promote the peace negotiations, which begin in a few days, by influencing his friends. The Bolsheviks are fighting, according to reliable reports, against growing internal difficulties and therefore have every interest in strengthening their position by an early peace.

BUSSCHE

---

[1] On the same day, Bussche sent a telegram (No. 1736, AS 4929 in WK 2 secr, volume 54) to Stockholm requesting the Minister there to ask Helphand to go to Copenhagen and then to Berlin.

109

The Minister in Stockholm to the Foreign Ministry

TELEGRAM NO. 2065

AS 5008

18 December 1917, 7.15 p.m.
Received: 18 December, 9.55 p.m.

Parvus would like, unless the matter is urgent, to stay here over Christmas, because of talks with Radek and Fürstenberg, who will be returning from Petrograd. Please telegraph instructions. Riezler.

LUCIUS

110

The Under State Secretary to the Minister in Stockholm

TELEGRAM NO. 1750

AS 5008

Berlin, 19 December 1917

In reply to telegram No. 2065.

For Riezler. It seems to me expedient to keep Parvus away from Stockholm because of the negotiations for the preliminary peace, which begin in the next few days. Please ask him once more to come here via Copenhagen.

BUSSCHE

111

The Counsellor of Legation in Stockholm to Minister Bergen

AS 5133

24 December 1917

Dear Herr von Bergen,

After having been unable to get a ticket for several days, Parvus is now leaving today. I enclose a memorandum about the part he has been playing recently.

At this moment, when his interests and ours are running parallel again, he is once more very important, and I would strongly recommend you to ask him, in confidence and quite intimately, for his advice in Berlin, especially on the Rumanian question (Rakovsky's future role, &c.). He really is a very considerable man and he has excellent ideas. It may well be that we shall soon feel that it would be an advantage to base our position in Russia on wider circles than those around Lenin, and in that event he will be essential to us.

He must not be allowed to suspect that we simply wanted to get him away from here.

I have nothing against his return, especially if things go well at Brest. However, I think that we could now use him better somewhere else, as Stockholm will soon cease to be of any importance as regards Russia because of the poor communications with Petrograd—that is, if nothing goes wrong at Brest. Let us hope that all goes well. It is difficult to judge from here, as the Radeks, &c., are apparently spinning some international revolutionary web of their own.

Best wishes and a happy Christmas.

Yours, &c.,
RIEZLER

Enclosure: Secret Memorandum

When he arrived here in the middle of November, Parvus at first certainly believed in the possibility and the usefulness of a Socialist conference. The Danish offer to convene such a conference, which has in the meanwhile shown no results and been forgotten, must be seen as the product of his efforts, and the same is true of the original co-operative attitude of the German Social Democrats towards the idea of a conference. The various aspects of his activities here were not really all very clear. Apart from his wish for a Socialist conference, he also hoped that the negotiations would move here or to Copenhagen, so that he could use his influence to control them on both sides. How far his influence over the Russian Socialists extends is not clear. He himself waited anxiously for news on this subject at first, and he now believes that Trotsky is openly and actively against him and Lenin neutral, but that the minor spirits are on his side. His assumption about Trotsky is certainly right, but Lenin may well also be against him, and he may have overestimated his influence on the others, just as he overestimated Vorovski's and Radek's confidence in him. He says that neither of these two makes a move without his knowledge. I have found out quite

definitely that he is totally mistaken in this supposition. Vorovski
is extremely suspicious of him and says that nobody really trusts
him. Dr. Helphand is now working to strengthen his position
in Russia, with the help of the 'Under-officers', in spite of Lenin
and Trotsky and even against them if necessary. In these circumstances and while preserving a relationship of confidence
with him in every way, I have had to eliminate him from all
questions concerned with methods for negotiation.

In all other questions, where his interests run parallel with
ours, he is extremely valuable by virtue of his great practical
political abilities, his exceptional knowledge of revolutionary
Russia and his strength of personality. His advice and help can
be of quite extraordinary value.

112

Report from Herr Nasse

AS 5184   Berlin, 26 December 1917

There is no doubt that there is a strong movement in the present
Russian government which is working to prevent the peace
negotiations which have already begun from coming to an end
too quickly. One important reason for this is the wish not to
antagonize the Entente too far; the other is the still existing
hope that a revolution will break out in Germany, which would
put the whole peace question on a different, and, for the Bolsheviks, far more advantageous basis.

The wish to maintain fairly good relations with the Entente
has grown stronger lately for several reasons; its great influence,
especially among the Russian bourgeoisie, and partly also
among the right-wing Socialists is directed, in the last analysis,
towards the frustration of the separate peace, and perhaps still
more towards the destruction of German-Russian trade.

It must be continually pointed out to the Russians that in
this respect, also, the Entente is pursuing selfish ends; only Germany—because of her geographical position—is capable of
assisting Russia to restore her economy quickly and effectively.

Furthermore, the Russian government should be made to
realize that it would only harm itself by vaccilation and long-
drawn-out negotiations, as all the above-mentioned endeavours
of the Entente would have to take place parallel to the restora-

tion of a bourgeois government. At any rate, the Bolshevik government realizes that the Kadets and the right-wing Socialists are working hard against them in secret; Radek told my confidential agent in Stockholm that they knew all about these activities and that when the moment came they would not hesitate to take firm measures; they would not suffer from the weaknesses of a Kerenski. The government was not entirely blind to the fact that in spite of its good police organization and its firm will to suppress counter-revolution, such movements can be highly injurious to it, especially while the government is not completely secure from the outside.

The second factor which makes for procrastination is the hope of an early revolution in Germany. How far the Bolshevik leaders in fact believe in this is difficult to tell; certain contemptuous remarks of Radek's about the German Independents, may justify the conclusion that he himself does not rely on them to any great extent. But even here the wish may be father to the thought: one must not forget the fact that the Bolsheviks have often declared that peace is their aim; not, however, peace achieved through negotiations with bourgeois governments, but through a kindling of revolution in our country as well, which would naturally lead to peace. According to my information the Independents have succeeded in sending a message to Stockholm urging that the peace negotiations, which would have a destructive effect on their hopes of a revolution should be abandoned; and if Radek and his friends interpret this attempt as sign of our weakness one cannot tell what kind of effect it may have on the decisions of the Russian government.

Naturally, I took pains to make it clear to my confidential agent that he should use his influence as far as this point was concerned, not only to represent these attempts of the Independents as harmful to the real interests of the government in Petrograd, but also to make it clear that, according to his knowledge, the situation in Germany does not warrant any hope of an early revolution.

Radek told my confidential agent that Germany was pressing for peace for two reasons: Germany wanted to launch a great offensive in the West in February 1918 and to have her rear free once and for all; but the main reason was that the water was already up to her neck. This became clear not only from the fact that the Central Powers negotiated so willingly with the revolutionary Bolshevik government, but also from the manner in which they joined the negotiations. Members of the Foreign

Ministry arrived at Brest-Litovsk in large numbers; from this the Bolsheviks could draw valuable conclusions. The Austrians in particular were so charming, so polite, and so anxious to oblige that they obviously made their German friends apprehensive. Behind every Austrian a Prussian planted himself, to make sure that their Allies did not go too far in their offers and promises.

Russian attempts, which are now recurring, to transfer the negotiations from Brest-Litovsk to a neutral country should be traced mainly to the influence of Radek and his friends, who may be pursuing a twofold aim. On the one hand, they hope that, if Stockholm, for instance, were chosen, they might gain greater influence, because then those men who for many months had been the representatives of the Bolsheviks in Stockholm would play a more important role in the negotiations. On the other hand, they perhaps hope for longer negotiations; in Stockholm the influence of the revolutionary Social Democracy, especially of the German group, would be more powerfully felt than in Petrograd, not to mention Brest-Litovsk. It is worth mentioning in this connexion that Radek's interest in the outbreak of the revolution is of an entirely different sort from that of Lenin and Trotsky.

It is interesting to note the following remark that Radek made: he said that he knew what the Lithuanian delegation in Berlin was promised, not by the Foreign Ministry, but by a general, who read to the delegation a telegram from Hindenburg agreeing to their independence but stipulating a common army and railway.[1]

[1] Bergen's marginal note: 'For the Under State Secretary; a report from Herr Nasse. I have sent a copy to Rosenberg.' Rosenberg was at Brest-Litovsk at the time.

113

The Deputy State Secretary to the Minister in Stockholm

TELEGRAM NO. 20

A 432   Berlin, 4 January 1918

For Riezler.

The latest publications of the Petersburg Telegraph Agency make it necessary to have serious words with Vorovski. They contain appeals to our nation, which include revolutionary matter, and calls to our soldiers to disobey orders and lay down their arms. This we must regard as improper and intolerable interference in our internal affairs. At the same time, libels are being published about us. We are portrayed as slave-drivers and oppressors of the workers. It is claimed that we put the workers' leaders into German concentration camps and that we appease the hunger of women and old men with lead and gunpowder. These lies apparently emanate from the Austrian Radek. It is surely impossible, in the long run, for a government which is engaged in peace negotiations with us, to use this kind of language about us in its publications, for these publications ultimately force one to doubt whether the Bolshevik government is serious in its wish to reach an understanding with us.

Instead of securing peace for Russia, and, with it, the necessary conditions for further development, their procrastination of the peace settlement is simply playing into the hands of the Entente, and they are doing harm to their own country by wasting valuable time in fruitless revolutionary agitation.[1]

BUSSCHE

[1] The same text was dispatched to Rosenberg at Brest-Litovsk as telegram No. 18 (Russland Nr. 61, volume 139).

114

The Deputy State Secretary to the Foreign Ministry Representative at Eastern Command

TELEGRAM NO. 114

AS 89   Berlin, 9 January 1918

For the State Secretary at Brest-Litovsk.

The Imperial Minister in Copenhagen has informed us of the contents of a letter from a Russian Social Revolutionary who is close to Chernov, to his friend in Copenhagen. This letter said that the Bolsheviks were now isolated, both morally and politically. The whole economic system and the Russian state were completely disorganized. The Bolsheviks would no more be able to maintain their power if they concluded peace, than if they failed to do so. The forces on which they were depending consisted only of a few hundred thousand soldiers. Moreover, the Bolsheviks had no followers among the intellectuals or among the democratic parties. Lenin had tried to bring about a unification at the last moment, by taking up the sixty-year-old agrarian programme of the Social Revolutionaries. The Social Revolutionaries, however, had remained true to their old principles and were now convinced that social reforms in all aspects of the Russian system could not be imposed by acts of violence. For this reason, the Social Revolutionaries would openly oppose the Bolsheviks, as soon as they were morally and physically capable of doing so.

Russia could only be saved by the Constituent Assembly, and a conflict of considerable violence would break out on the subject of this very Assembly. The intellectuals, the Social Revolutionaries and even some of the soldiers would stop at nothing in this conflict, and even the troops, or rather the socially conscious nucleus of the troops would abandon Lenin.

People who had languished for thirty to forty years in Russian prisons or in Siberia had once again been thrown into jail by the Bolsheviks because of their political convictions. Even members of the Constituent Assembly which has now been elected, who, of course, are supposed to enjoy immunity, were lying in prison. The laws had been declared invalid and there was no legal code at all in Russia. Tribunals consisting of Bolsheviks were functioning as courts of law. The entire press was under pressure. Those newspapers that still appeared were censored before publication, and even the organs of the extreme left were being gagged in this way. Newspapers were simply closed down and their types, their paper, and their capital confiscated.

Chernov held exactly the same view and stood in the centre of the movement which wanted to oppose the Bolsheviks. The next task for the Social Revolutionary party, and indeed for all Russians except the Bolsheviks, would be to hold organized meetings of soldiers, and this was already being done where possible. In addition, special newspapers, leaflets, and weekly bulletins were to be published.

All Russia was following the course of the negotiations at Brest-Litovsk with fevered interest, but there was no agreement with the leadership. The German interpretation of the formula 'Peace without annexations or reparations' was unacceptable to all the non-Leninist elements in Russia, for the thinking Democrats, i.e. the Democrats of the future, read an undertone of dictation to a defeated Russia into the negotiations.

The organization of plebiscites in the occupied territories was regarded as part of the internal affairs of Russia, not of Germany. The Russians had the impression that the delegations from Lithuania, the Baltic, &c., were simply carrying out orders.

The conclusion of a peace such as the one now threatening could set only one aim for all Russian Democrats, namely mobilization, for Russia could not exist without the Baltic provinces. The Balts themselves also wanted to remain Russian, and the 9 per cent. of Germans could play no decisive role in this matter.

A democratic peace need not be concluded by Lenin alone; it could alternatively be concluded by him (i.e. by Lenin as the embodiment of Socialist demagogy) in collaboration with the Democratic element.

If the German people really wanted to adopt a brotherly attitude towards the Russian people, then it would have to abandon all ideas of diplomatic self-interest and conclude an honest peace. Otherwise Russia would be forced to remobilize, and in thirty years there would be another war.

The senior Social Revolutionary in question believes that the Germans in no way agree with his views because he is not on the side of the Bolsheviks. He therefore thinks that, for the moment, there is nothing that he can do which would at one and the same time reflect the wishes of the Germans and his own.

Should we share his views, then this Social Revolutionary would perhaps be prepared to make an active attempt to bring our mutual aims nearer fulfilment. In his opinion, the Bolsheviks would fall at the first shock, and he would not require large funds to bring this about.

In connexion with this man's remarks, it should be noted that Chernov has lost much of his influence since the rise of the left wing of the Social Revolutionaries under Spiridonova. If Your Excellency approves, I intend to tell him that, at the moment, we are unfortunately not in a position to take up relations with other Russian parties, as we are engaged in negotiations with the Bolsheviks. Please inform me of your views by telegram.[1]

BUSSCHE

[1] Reply from the State Secretary: 'I agree. Kühlmann. (A 5133 in WK 2 secr, volume 56. Telegram No. 74 of 10 January 1918.)

115

The Minister in Copenhagen to the Foreign Ministry

TELEGRAM NO. 37

A 1512   11 January 1918, 12.30 a.m.
Received: 11 January, 5.18 a.m.

A telegram from the Danish Minister in Petrograd, in approximately the following terms, arrived here today:

On Monday the English Ambassador left, saying that his mind had ceased to function properly and that he was a completely broken man.

The rumours of the departure of the French Ambassador are, to say the least, premature. However, it is true that a conflict has arisen between the representatives of France and the Bolsheviks. A young French officer spread the rumour that the Germans had demanded the surrender of the Black Sea fleet, and this report caused great excitement. The French Ambassador has stated that the officer would be relieved of his post.

Differences have also arisen with the Rumanian representatives. Trotsky is complaining of the strict measures taken by the Rumanian government against Bolshevik propaganda.

The representatives of Germany and Austria are being closely watched. They may only move in the streets if accompanied by soldiers, and their correspondence is censored.[1] The real reason for this probably lies in Trotsky's fear that the German representatives might make contact with anti-revolutionary circles here—and the sympathies of these circles definitely lie on the side of the Germans.

There is little intention to reach any positive results in the Austro-German commission. The negotiations have adopted the form of meetings in which all sorts of matters are debated.[2]

BROCKDORFF-RANTZAU

---

[1] The German economic and naval missions arrived in Petrograd on 29 December 1917, headed by Mirbach and Rear Admiral Keyserling. At Brest-Litovsk the Russian delegates stressed the humanitarian function of the mission: it was to discuss and settle the question of interned civil prisoners, the exchange of disabled prisoners of war and similar problems.

The activities of the mission remained within the limits agreed upon at Brest-Litovsk. (The relevant documents can be found in the series Russland Politisches Nr. 1a.) From time to time Mirbach reported on the desolation of the Russian capital and predicted an early fall of the Bolshevik government. The missions left Petrograd on 18 February and on 23 February Mirbach and Keyserling reported to the Kaiser at General Headquarters. Mirbach returned to Russia as the German Minister at the end of April. He presented his credentials to Sverdlov on 26 April.

² The Kaiser's marginal remark: 'That is the passion of the Russians! Energetic measures will have to be taken and *la duce violence* exercised' [*sic*]. (The Kaiser probably meant: *la douce violence*.)

116

The Foreign Ministry Representative in Petrograd to the Chancellor

REPORT NO. 26

A 4166   Petrograd, 24 January 1918

An identical report has been sent to the State Secretary.

Judging by purely external signs, the power of the Bolsheviks seems to have secured itself to some extent during the last few days. Whether or how long this positive trend will last remains to be seen. Since political life here moves entirely in convulsive spasms, one must always be prepared to reckon with very brief stages.

For the moment, however, the big planned coups of the Smolny government have been successful. Since it depended on the support of the Red Guard and of marines—rather than on the army proper—and thus had control of the streets, it was not very difficult for the government to send the Constituent Assembly, whose opening looks more and more like a farce, home after little more than twenty-four hours and, in place of this unacceptable body, to summon the Convention, which supports the government unconditionally.

In all other fields, too, the government is following the well-tried formula: 'If you won't be my brother I'll beat your brains in.' The press could hardly be more completely gagged. With the exception of the party organs *Pravda* and *Izvestia*, all the newspapers are strictly censored and, if necessary, severely punished.¹ Political opponents, too, enjoy short shrift. Politicians, deputies, editors, and other such members of the opposition live under a continual threat to their liberty, if not worse. Those arrested last week include Shamanski, the president of the Red Cross. There is no means of knowing how many other people may have shared this fate, as only very few cases are admitted publicly and the government presumably 'works' mainly in secret.

The great sensation of the last few days was the murder of the ex-Ministers Shingarev and Kokoshkin. Because of their poor state of health, these two men had been taken from the Fortress of SS. Peter and Paul to a hospital, where they were shot by marines on the night after their admission. Kokoshkin was shot dead, but Shingarev only died after several hours suffering. At first sight, the crime bore all the marks of a simple political murder, but the governing clique denies any complicity, claiming that, on the contrary, the murder was contrived by the opposition in order to secure for themselves a weapon against the Bolsheviks.

MIRBACH

¹ The Kaiser's marginal remark: 'We shall have to do the same with our gutter-press.'

117

The Deputy State Secretary to the Foreign Ministry Representative at Eastern Command

TELEGRAM NO. 478

A 4886   Berlin, 2 February 1918

Dr. Helphand, who spoke here at discussions about the situation inside Russia, is of the opinion that our relations with the Bolsheviks must be handled with the greatest care. He believes that the Bolsheviks' ideas will spread still further in Russia and that the [Ukrainian] Rada will not last much longer.

He said that nobody would be able to drive out the Bolsheviks, now that they had occupied the Donetz basin and Kharkov, the centre of the industrial Ukraine, except with the help of German troops.

Helphand still thinks that there is a possibility of the Bolsheviks forming a coalition with the left wing of the Social Revolutionary party.

BUSSCHE

118

The Deputy State Secretary to the State Secretary (in Bucharest)

TELEGRAM NO. 99

AS 1202   Berlin, 7 March 1918

Count Roedern wishes to garnish his latest credit demands, which he will be presenting to the Reichstag next week, with a few comments on foreign policy in order to enliven the atmosphere a little, and would be grateful to Your Excellency for some suitable hints. Would you please give me the necessary instructions?

BUSSCHE

119

The State Secretary to the Foreign Ministry

TELEGRAM NO. 88

AS 1261   Bucharest, 11 March 1918, 11.45 a.m.
                                   Received: 11 March, 12.45 p.m.

In answer to telegram No. 99.

The overall situation is so uncertain that I should advise against making any comments on foreign policy, if not absolutely necessary. In view of the latest reports from Russia, and of the opposition to the ratification of our treaties which exists there, I would especially recommend moderation in the evaluation of the positive results achieved at Brest. One could probably say that the Eastern sky was beginning to lighten, but it would perhaps be better not, as yet, to assume that the transition from war on two fronts to war on a single front is definitely assured.

KÜHLMANN

120

The Minister in Moscow to the Chancellor

REPORT NO. 9

A 19757   30 April 1918

In the hands of the Bolsheviks, Moscow, the sacred city, the embodiment of the power of the Tsars, the high place of the Orthodox Church, represents what is perhaps the most glaring destruction of taste and style that has resulted from the Russian revolution.[1] Any one who knew the capital in the days of its glory would hardly be able to recognize it now. In every part of the city, and especially in the central commercial quarter, countless bullet-holes in walls and windows are evidence of the bitter battles which were fought for its possession. The great Hotel Metropol has been wrecked by artillery fire, and even the Kremlin has suffered terribly. Various of its gates are badly damaged; the Iberian Gate has been partly destroyed and is now only boarded up.

There is seething activity in the streets, but they seem to be exclusively populated by the proletariat. Hardly any better-dressed people are to be seen—as if the whole of the previous governing class and the bourgeoisie had disappeared from the face of the earth. This may be partly connected with the fact that most of them are trying to conform externally with the scene that has been set in the streets, so as not to inflame the lust for loot and the unpredictable temper of the class which now rules the city. The Orthodox priests, who used to form a considerable part of the public in the streets, have also disappeared from the scene. Hardly anything can be bought in the shops except dusty remnants of past splendour, and these only at fantastic prices. The hallmarks of the whole picture are general unwillingness to work and aimless loafing.[2] As the factories are still at a standstill and the land is still, to all intents and purposes, not being cultivated—at least this was the impression that I got on my journey—Russia seems to be heading for an even worse catastrophe than that already produced by the revolution.

Public safety leaves much to be desired, but one can now move about freely and alone by day. However, it is unwise to go out towards evening, and at that time of day one often hears rifle fire and more or less serious skirmishes seem to take place continually.

The old property-owning class is in a state of profoundest misery; it needs only a government order to strip them of all their possessions. Thus the ominous requisition order, which drives the owners on to the street, often at only a few hours' notice, can be seen hanging on almost all the palaces and the larger private houses.

The despair of the old governing classes is boundless, but they can no longer raise sufficient strength[3] to put an end to the organized lotting which is now prevalent. The cry for organized conditions reaches down to the lowest strata of the people, and the feeling of their own impotence makes them hope for salvation from Germany.[4] The very circles who were inveighing loudest against us before, now see us, if not as the Angel, then at least as the Police Constable of Salvation.

The rise in the price of food has been considerable, but as the pockets of the lower classes are stuffed with the billions of roubles printed by Kerenski, it is only the old property-owners who are living in misery. The eight-hour working-day has been generally introduced, and the minimum wages for domestic servants have been fixed at 200 roubles a month plus free board and lodging.

The supremacy of the Bolsheviks in Moscow is principally upheld by the Livonian battalions, and then also by the large number of motor vehicles requisitioned by the government, which rush continually around the town and can bring troops to danger-spots as required.

It is impossible to see where these conditions will lead; for the moment one can only say that they bid fair to remain much the same.

MIRBACH

[1] The Kaiser's marginal remark: 'This is not our concern; the world war lacks in style as well.'

[2] The Kaiser's marginal remark: 'The hall-mark of the "Social state of the future".'

[3] The Kaiser's marginal remark: 'This will have to come from the outside.'

[4] The Kaiser's marginal remark: 'Either England and America or *we* (indirectly through Russian generals).'

121

The Liaison Officer at General Headquarters to the Foreign Ministry

TELEGRAM NO. 1034

A 19341   6 May 1918, 9.30 p.m.
                     Received: 6 May, 10.30 p.m.

Eastern Command has sent the following telegram to High Command of the Army:

'A.O.K. 8 has telegraphed as follows:

Captain von Milinsky of the War Ministry, who is at the moment in Petrograd, instructed a courier who returned from Petrograd on 1 May (Lt. Brussatis) to tell the German Army Command the following:

"The Maximalist government was to be overthrown by the Minimalists, on the instigation and with the financial support of the French, the English, and the Americans. The appointed date, 1 May, had to be postponed because the organization was incomplete. The dictators of the Minimalist government were to be Chernov, General Schwarz, Kriwotshein, and Gavenko [*sic*] and also, supposedly, Kerenski in Petrograd. After the victory of the counter-revolution, an army of 30,000 to 50,000 men was to attack the German troops in Finland or Estonia, in order to ease the burden on the French front. The Maximalists were warned of the imminent counter-revolution by Monarchists and the Soviet government arranged for the arrest of the Minimalist dictators. A French firm is evacuating large quantities of metal, crude rubber, and motor tyres from Petrograd. German delegates were not able to seize this opportunity, as they had no authority to buy. Large and favourable offers were made to them."

'To make Lt. B[russatis]'s journey possible, a Russian officer, Georg, a delegate of Major-General Shulgin, accompanied him. Georg is at the disposal of the German government until 8 May for any commissions that may be required.'

BERCKHEIM

122

The Liaison Officer at General Headquarters to the Foreign Ministry

TELEGRAM NO. 1047

A 19596   8 May 1918, 12 noon.
                                   Received: 8 May, 1.40 p.m.

General Ludendorff would be grateful for information about Count Mirbach's reports on the internal political situation in Russia. The General thinks that it is not impossible that a government hostile to us might take over the helm and considers it advisable to prepare for this possibility by helping circles acceptable to us to take over the reins of government.

BERCKHEIM

123

The Minister in Moscow to the Foreign Ministry

TELEGRAM NO. 78

A 19966   10 May 1918, 11.59 p.m.
                                   Received: 11 May, 2.10 a.m.

I have heard from a good but not yet fully proven source that the representatives of the Entente countries here, under the chairmanship of Francis, yesterday approved an ultimatum to the Soviet Government, which they delivered today and in which the Entente solemnly offered to continue even now to support Russia with food, arms, and raw materials for its fight against Germany and held out hopes of the recognition of the Soviet government by the Entente in the event of general mobilization. Karachan and Radek did not tell me of this event, perhaps because the official reaction was not to be discussed until this evening. The conduct of the affairs of the Entente has been entirely transferred from Vologda on to the shoulders of the representatives here, who now receive instructions direct from their governments. The more prudent of the Bolshevik leaders are still trying to calm those elements which are incensed about the advance in the South and the restoration in the Ukraine. However, in view of the enormous worries of the Bolshevik government and its perplexity about the developments in the South, it is not impossible that there may be surprises.

I heard, after the event, that the Entente had this evening made further urgent approaches to Sverdlov with important offers to organize the transport of food from Siberia, and that the non-Bolshevik Socialist parties, also this evening and in line with the steps taken by the Entente, had offered to let bygones be bygones and to co-operate with the Bolsheviks for the salvation of Russia. I am continuing with my secret efforts to ensure the rejection of both offers.

MIRBACH

124

The Minister in Moscow to the Foreign Ministry

TELEGRAM NO. 96

A 20377

13 May 1918, 6.50 p.m.
Received: 13 May, 9.00 p.m.

In continuation of telegram No. 78.

As far as can be judged from the opinions, the attitudes and the strengths of the various political strata and from the overall situation, it appears to me, as I see it from here, that our interests still demand the continuation in power of the Bolshevik government. [*One word garbled*] the efforts at insinuation and the professions of friendship of all the other parties, there is, in most cases, only the wish to be rid of the Bolsheviks. If they do fall, then all their successors will with the aid of the Entente, work for reunification with the ceded territories, especially with the Ukraine, and for the revision of the Brest peace treaty. Any further advance on our part might drive the Bolsheviks into the arms of the Entente or, in the event of their fall, bring successors favourable to the Entente into power. In the event of relations with us being broken off, an event which in that case could hardly be avoided, the leadership in Russian political and economic development would fall to the Entente. As far as can be seen from here, it would best serve our interests to continue to provide the Bolsheviks with a minimum of essential goods and to maintain them in power. In spite of all their decrees, something can probably be achieved with the Bolsheviks for the present time, for they are now all of a sudden much more co-operative again in economic affairs, and at least some prepara-tions can be made for future economic infiltration.

MIRBACH

125

Protocol of a Meeting at Spa, 13 May 1918

AS 2230

Greater Russia[1]

State Secretary von Kühlmann explained that the Entente had apparently recently approached the Bolsheviks with promises, if the latter would reopen the war against Germany. He did not consider this alarming from a military point of view. The Bol-sheviks were in any case under a severe threat from the left, i.e. from a party which paid homage to even more radical views than the Bolsheviks, who seemed to be trying gradually to orientate themselves towards the right. It would, at all events, be very much in our interests if it could be announced, once and for all, that our operations in Russia were definitely finished.

General Ludendorff replied that this was now the case and that it had presumably already been announced.

At the General's request, Colonel von Winterfeldt stated that he had told Under State Secretary von den Bussche that the demarcation-line was being drawn and that the advance had thus reached its conclusion.

General Ludendorff added that our troops were very often attacked by bands of Bolsheviks and other Russian groups, and that fighting therefore kept breaking out again, even against our wish. In any case, the Bolsheviks had long ceased to be what they were when they first made their appearance. They were now actively occupied with the idea of setting up an army and had already got some troops together. In internal politics, too, their attitude had really changed considerably, as the State Secretary of the Foreign Ministry had explained.

---

[1] Only the last part of the protocol is printed here. The discussion begins with the Ukrainian problem, then the Caucasus, the Dobrudja question, Alsace-Lorraine, the Flemmish movement, and the Crimea.

126

The Minister in Moscow to the Foreign Ministry

TELEGRAM NO. 114

A 20759
15 May 1918
Dispatched: 16 May, 1.45 p.m.
Received: 16 May, 4.30 p.m.

Chicherin today asked for a preliminary discussion on economic questions with Bronski, the Minister of Commerce. Bronski set out an extensive programme for the economic opening-up of Russia, of which the bases are contained in the telegram which was openly passed on to Joffe at Chicherin's request.[1] Chicherin added that these economic suggestions presupposed a settlement of political questions such as would not completely throttle Russia. The Russians ask that the negotiations of the commission in Moscow be speeded up and suggest that it would be more practical to have one commission dealing with questions of law and reparations, another with financial questions, and a third with questions of commerce, economics, and concessions. I therefore recommend that negotiations be begun on this basis as soon as possible, but that nobody with a personal interest in the restoration of former Russian economic conditions be invited to take part.

MIRBACH

[1] Telegram No. 113 (A 20704 in Deutschland Nr. 131, volume 38).

127

The Minister in Moscow to the Chancellor

REPORT NO. 61

A 21421
16 May 1918

Today I had a fairly long discussion with Lenin about the overall situation.

In general, Lenin trusts his lucky star with the utmost conviction and repeatedly expresses the most boundless optimism in an almost overpowering way. However, he does admit that, even though his system is still standing firm, the number of his opponents has increased and that the situation 'demands intenser vigilance than it did a month ago'.

He bases his faith principally on the fact that the governing party is the only one which has any organized force at its disposal, whereas all the others only agree in their opposition to the present system whilst, beyond this, they diverge in all directions and have no power behind them to equal that of the Bolsheviks.[1]

In some respects this is certainly true, but the tone in which Lenin speaks of the impotence of his enemies shows that he nevertheless somewhat underestimates them.

Beyond this, however, Lenin quite freely admits that his opponents are no longer to be found exclusively among the parties on his right, but that they are now also being recruited in his own camp, where a kind of left wing has formed. The main complaint of this opposition inside his own house is that the treaty of Brest-Litovsk, which he is still determined to defend with the utmost tenacity, was a mistake. More and more Russian territory was being occupied; the peace with Finland and the Ukraine had still not been ratified; the famine had not merely not been vanquished, but was actually on the increase. In short, a state of peace worthy of the name was still apparently in the far distance.

Unfortunately he had to admit that certain events in the recent past seemed to justify the attacks of his opponents. It was for this reason that he was directing all his desires and efforts towards a speedy clarification of matters in the North and the South,[2] and particularly towards achieving a peace settlement with Helsinki and Kiev, with the help of our co-operation and influence.[3]

Not that Lenin spoke plaintively or querulously, nor did he insinuate in any way that, if the present state of affairs were to last, he might be forced to turn back towards the other powers. However, he was quite apparently concerned to describe the awkwardness of his position as graphically as possible.[4]

MIRBACH

---

[1] The Kaiser's marginal remark: 'The Japanese, the Chinese, the English!? He will have the whole Kossack army against him!'

[2] The Kaiser's marginal remark: 'The Kossack army will settle that soon.'

[3] The Kaiser's marginal remark: 'He will be as unable to put these conditions into practice as those of Brest. He has neither government nor executive personnel.'

[4] The Kaiser's marginal remark: 'He is finished.'

128

The Minister in Moscow to the Foreign Ministry

TELEGRAM NO. 122

A 20991   16 May 1918
Dispatched: 17 May, 10.30 p.m.
Received: 18 May, 1.25 a.m.

According to a reliable source, situation in Petrograd once
again precarious. The Entente is supposed to be spending enormous sums in order to put right-wing Social Revolutionaries
into power and reopen war. The sailors on board the ships *Res
Publica* and *Zarya Rosii*, and on the cruiser *Oleg*, which has sailed
to Ino, are said to have been bribed with large sums; likewise
the former Preobrazhenski Regiment. Stores of arms in Sestro-
retck armament works in the hands of Social Revolutionaries.
Bolsheviks cannot find central office of this apparently well-
conducted organization. The movement is supposed to have
opened relations with Dutov and the Siberian movement. Here,
too, agitation has increased. I am still trying to counter efforts
of the Entente and support the Bolsheviks. However, I would
be grateful for instructions as to whether overall situation justi-
fies use of larger sums in our interests if necessary, and as to what
trend to support in event of Bolsheviks being incapable of holding out. If Bolsheviks fall, successors [*one word garbled*] to Entente
have best prospects at the moment.   MIRBACH

129

The State Secretary to the Minister in Moscow

TELEGRAM NO. 121

A 20991   Berlin, 18 May 1918
In reply to telegram No. 122.

Please use larger sums, as it is greatly in our interests that Bolsheviks should survive. Riezler's funds at your disposal. If further
money required, please telegraph how much. It is very difficult
to say from here which trend to support if Bolsheviks fall. If

really hard-pressed, left-wing Social Revolutionaries would fall with Bolsheviks. These parties seem to be the only ones who base their position on peace treaty of Brest-Litovsk. As a party, Kadets are anti-German; Monarchists would also work for revision of Brest peace treaty. We have no interest in supporting Monarchists' ideas, which would reunite Russia. On the contrary, we must try to prevent Russian consolidation as far as possible and, from this point of view, we must therefore support the parties furthest to the left.

KÜHLMANN

130

The State Secretary to the Minister in Moscow

TELEGRAM NO. 246

A 23074   Berlin, 1 June 1918

We have heard from the liaison officer of the High Command of the Army in Finland that Polish and Czech troops are being moved to the Murmansk railway for transport to the Western front. We have also heard from a reliable source that five trainloads of fully equipped Serbs have been seen on the line from Vologda to Perm. It must be made clear to the government in Moscow that we cannot stand by and watch such undertakings on the part of the Entente. If the Russian government should be incapable of effectively preventing such troop transports from taking place, then we should have to seek more extensive guarantees against any support being sent to the Entente by way of the Murmansk coast. Your Excellency will be informed as soon as we receive a reply from the High Command of the Army to the suggestion that a German commissar be sent to the Murmansk area, but I would request you to discuss these events with Chicherin at once in whatever way you think best, to point out to him the gravity of the matter, and to tell him that this state of affairs cannot possibly be allowed to continue. Finally, according to other reports, a Czechoslovak corps has passed through Chabarovsk. We insist that it be prevented from travelling on to Vladivostok, should such a move be intended. Report by telegram.

KÜHLMANN

131

The Minister in Moscow to the Foreign Ministry

TELEGRAM NO. 233

A 23614

3 June 1918, 5.41 p.m.
Received: 4 June, 3.20 a.m.

Due to strong Entente competition, 3,000,000 marks per month
necessary. In event of early need for change in our political line,
a higher sum must be reckoned with.   MIRBACH

132

The Counsellor of Legation in Moscow to Minister Bergen

AS 2655

4 June 1918

Dear Herr von Bergen,
In the last two weeks, the situation has very rapidly come to a
head. Famine is on the way, and is being choked off with terror.
The pressure exerted by the Bolsheviks' mailed fist is enormous.
People are being quietly shot by the hundred. All this, in itself,
is not so bad, but there can no longer be any doubt that the
physical means with which the Bolsheviks are maintaining their
power are running out. Supplies of petrol for motor vehicles are
coming to an end, and even the Latvian soldiers sitting in the
vehicles are no longer absolutely reliable—not to mention the
peasants and the workers. The Bolsheviks are extremely nervous
and can feel their end approaching, and all the rats are therefore beginning to leave the sinking ship. Nobody can tell how
they will face their end, and their dying agony may last several
more weeks. Perhaps they will try to flee to Nizhni or to Ekaterin-
burg. Perhaps they intend to fall in their own blood, like desperate men, or perhaps to invite us to leave in order to be rid of
the treaty of Brest—'the breathing space', as they call it—and
with it their compromise with typical imperialism, thus salving
their revolutionary consciences in their dying moments. These
people are completely incalculable, especially in their despair.
In addition, they once again believe that the more and more un-

disguised 'military dictatorship' in Germany is encountering enormous opposition, especially as a result of the further advance in the East, and that it is bound to lead to the revolution. Sokolnikov wrote this recently, apparently on the basis of Joffe's reports.

For the moment their terror seems to have gained them a little wind, but, in spite of this, Karakhan has put the original of the treaty of Brest ready in his desk. He intends to take the document with him to America and to sell it, with the Emperor's signature on it, to the highest bidder.

The moans and whines of the bourgeoisie for German aid and order need not move us, but we must nevertheless reckon with one serious possibility—namely the possibility of the resurrection of a reasonably ordered bourgeois Russia with the help of the Entente. There are Czechoslovak troops here; there are English and French in Archangel and Massnau, and there are officers' associations and party organizations. Joy at liberation from the terror of the Bolsheviks might help the country over some of its economic problems, and the reopening of the banks and of free commerce might considerably alleviate matters. If that were to happen, then the Ukraine of the Kiev Kadets and Skoropadski would throw off the last of its Ukrainian veils and become one with Greater Russia. We should then be in the awkward position of either having to face an irresistible movement with a few divisions, or of being forced to accept it. Surely we must prepare ourselves to anticipate this. In concrete terms, that means that we must spin a thread reaching to Orenburg and Siberia over General Krasnov's head, hold cavalry, directed at Moscow but concealed, ready for any eventuality, prepare a future government here with which we could agree, dipping as deep as possible into the ranks of the Kadets for it (in order, if necessary, to compromise them too), and finally revise those terms of the treaty of Brest directed against economic hegemony within Russia as a whole, i.e. reunite the Ukraine with Russia and make something out of Estonia and Livonia which we could later sell back to Russia. To facilitate the restoration of a Russia which would again be imperialist is not a pleasant perspective, but this development may perhaps be inevitable, for, in view of the total instability of the Rada (that is, as far as I and everybody else here see it), any idea of a lasting independence for the Ukraine would now only be a fantasy and, in spite of everything, the vitality of the united Russian soul is enormous. The Ukraine would fall with the Bolsheviks. The *fait accompli* of a dynasty in

Kiev might slightly lengthen the life of this artificial state, but nothing more. As far as my work here is concerned, the apparatus of our united rivals, who are working in a variety of roles, is extremely powerful, and our devalued roubles disappear at a rapid rate.

Please forgive this personal effusion about a state of chaos which, even viewed from here, is all too impenetrable.

With best wishes,
Yours, &c.,
RIEZLER

4 June

P.S. Things look a little better today. The terror seems to be having its effect and appears seriously to have disturbed the conspiracy which had been prepared. There is still hunger, which grows more and more threatening, and since people imagine the South full of grain, we are being blamed, and not without some justification, for the shortage of bread, petrol, and coal. We *might* nevertheless have another six or eight weeks in which to consider whether we can risk a state of chaos inclined towards the Entente, from which we should be excluded economically, or whether, for the sake of the natural resources, &c. we shall have to decide to set up a bourgeois order with which we can reach agreement.

133

The State Secretary of the Foreign Ministry to the State Secretary of the Treasury

Berlin, 8 June 1918

AS 2562

Dear Rödern,

I herewith enclose, for your personal and strictly confidential information, a memorandum in which you can read of all the latest developments. I will send the official application, with no reasons stated, as soon as I have your agreement in principle. In view of the great importance of this matter, I should be especially grateful for an early favourable reply.

Yours, &c.,
KÜHLMANN

Enclosure: Memorandum for the State Secretary, for discussion with Count Rödern

Berlin, 5 June 1918

During the most recent efforts of the Entente in Russia to persuade the Soviet of the Workers' Delegates to accept the demands of the Entente, an acceptance which would result in the orientation of Russia towards the Entente, Count Mirbach was forced to spend considerable sums in order to prevent any resolution to this effect.

The Bolsheviks have, for the moment, been successfully restrained from steering into the waters of the Entente, but every day may bring new surprises. The Social Revolutionaries have completely sold themselves to the Entente which, with the help of the Czechoslovak battalions, is trying to undermine the supremacy of the Bolsheviks. It appears that the Bolsheviks have, for the moment, succeeded in overcoming the attack of the Czechoslovak troops. Nevertheless, the next few months will be taken up with internal political strife. This may possibly even lead to the fall of the Bolsheviks, especially as one or two of their leaders have already reached a certain degree of resignation as to their own fate.

As long as the Bolshevik government remains in power, we shall have to try to apply every available means to keep the Bolsheviks from orientating themselves in any other direction, in spite of the severe tests and handicaps which our own political demands (Estonia, Livonia, Transcaucasia, Crimea, &c.) will impose on them. This will cost money; probably a great deal of money. On the other hand, as we are already reckoning with the possibility of the overthrow of the Bolsheviks, we must not break off relations with the other political parties. On the contrary, we must assure ourselves a transition as free of danger as possible, should the Bolsheviks fall. This too will cost money.

Count Mirbach has reported that he will now need 3 million marks a month for expenses on these activities. In the event of a change of policy, however, double this sum may well be needed, circumstances permitting.

The fund which we have so far had at our disposal for acquisitions in Russia is exhausted. It is therefore essential that the Secretary of the Imperial Treasury put a new fund at our disposal. In view of the conditions set out above, this fund will have to amount to at least 40 million marks.

TRAUTMANN[1]

[1] Counsellor in the Foreign Ministry.

134

The First Quartermaster General to the State Secretary

A 252028   General Headquarters, 9 June 1918

Will your Excellency allow me to express my views on our military and political position in the East? Because of the shortage of manpower we have had to weaken our divisions there still further. They are strong enough to carry out their duties of occupation, but should the situation in the East deteriorate, their strength will not be sufficient. In any case, because of the obscure policy of the weak Soviet government, we must look round for other allies in the East. In the North we have Finland, which has strengthened its military position as a result of our entry, completed with the approval of Your Excellency. We may hope that we shall find strong military support there whatever happens.

The Ukraine has not yet been successful in building up its own army. Ukraine is essential to our survival and to our supply of raw materials. From the military point of view we are justified to use our troops there; it would be a mistake to do otherwise.

In Georgia, as in Finland, we have the opportunity of strengthening our fighting forces; we must organize a Georgian army. It is therefore necessary to recognize and protect the Georgian state. An ethical point should be taken into consideration in this case; Georgia is a Christian state whose hopes we have been raising for a long time. Germany's recognition and protection will at the same time give Georgia security against the greedy Turks. Otherwise the difficulties there will never be over. I beg you to examine M. Chenkeli's full powers while he is with you and to carry out the policy I have suggested to ensure that Georgia, like Finland, should support our war effort. We should not postpone taking decisions until the first reports of General Kress[1] have reached us. If Georgia is our advanced base, it is to be hoped that the Caucasian territory will be gradually pacified and that we should be able to draw from there the raw materials we so urgently need.

I should like to stress that Turkey must be taken into account and that we must, to a certain degree, regard its wishes. The railway line from Batum through Tiflis to Djulfa is extremely important to their operations. The transport of troops on this line must be made secure for Turkey. We should not forgo running the Tiflis–Baku line under German control. There the

Turks will have to give way to us. Also, Baku should not be ceded to the Turks. General Kress[1] will have first to find out what the situation is in the Armenian and the Tartar parts of Caucasia. The guiding principle should be that Turkey should not hinder the development of the Georgian army and the provision of raw materials from the Caucasus. It would be an act of hostility towards us if the Turks were to occupy the Tiflis–Baku line and Baku itself, an occupation which might lead to the destruction of the local oil industry.

It follows from all this that we can expect military support from Finland and Georgia in the East. That is not sufficient. We also have to enter into contact with the Caucasian Cossack tribes, which are trying to elude the grasp of the Soviet government. The return of arms apprehended by us would be a step in this direction, as long as we have a guarantee that they will not be used against us.

I believe that everything in the military field which our position in the East requires has been done; this is not so in the political field.

Here I regard the dishonourable endeavours of the Soviet government with the gravest distrust. I have expressed this to Your Excellency on several occasions. The enclosed telegram shows the attitude of this government in an exceptionally bad light. I would also like to remind you of the questions of the prisoners of war, the support of the Red Guard in Finland by the Soviet government, the preferential treatment of the Entente on the Murman railway, the boats in Novorosiisk, and the restoration of economic relations with us. Especially annoying is the attitude of the Soviet government towards the Czechoslovak, Serbian, and Rumanian troops, though M. Joffe disputes this. Instead of disarming them as agreed, the Soviet government either armed the Czechoslovak and other troops, or allowed them to go on as before, and even to fight against us in the Ukraine, in order to get to the Murman railway and leave for the Far East. From there—the Soviet government believed—they could be transported to France and fight against us. It seems to have corresponded to the wishes of the Entente to occupy the Murman and the East Siberian lines with these troops in order to dominate Russia. Then the Soviet government went through a volte-face and suddenly declared that the Czechoslovak troops wanted to disarm. Their mendacity thus came into the open.

I shall only mention here that the claims of the Soviet government increased as soon as they discovered that we would not cross the demarcation line, although they always protested against our alleged advance. The Soviet government has, as far as one can see, adopted the same attitude towards us as at the beginning of the negotiations at Brest. The Soviet government procrastinates as far as all the, for us, important decisions are concerned and works as often as it can against us. We can expect nothing from this government, although it lives by our mercy. It is a lasting danger to us which will diminish only when it recognizes us unconditionally as the supreme Power and becomes pliable through its fear of Germany and concern for its own existence. Therefore a strong and ruthless treatment of this government appears to me still to be indicated.

We have to see that our own demands, which our own position requires, are unconditionally and quickly complied with in order to avoid any unpleasant surprises in the East.

The Soviet government has not yet proved that it can rule its territory. So far it has destroyed, and now, turning sharply to the Right, it will build. But to do this, they have no administration. At any rate, there are powerful trends working against the Soviet government; we have to take note of these.

Though we now negotiate officially only with the Soviet government, we should at the same time entertain relations with other movements in Russia, in order not to find ourselves suddenly high and dry. We cannot rely on Kerensky's partisans, because they are dominated by the Entente. We have to acquire contacts with the right-wing monarchist groups and influence them so that the monarchist movement would be governed by our wishes as soon as it gained influence. The Entente has also recognized the importance of this movement. According to reliable information the Entente has already promised its support to the Monarchists through Minister Noulens at a meeting of conservative elements, and proposed the introduction of a constitutional monarchy. The proposal was acknowledged politely but so far has not been answered.

In the economic field we have to achieve clear agreements with the Russian nationalities, otherwise we shall run the danger of the Soviet government's doing everything in its power to improve on the Brest treaty. The economic agreements in the East should also dissolve the threats of the Entente as to the boycott of Germany; this will greatly strengthen our position at future peace negotiations, and in the whole world. LUDENDORFF

---

[1] General Kress led a military expedition to the Caucasus at the time.

135

The State Secretary of the Treasury to the State Secretary of the Foreign Ministry

AS 2667   Berlin, 11 June 1918

Dear Kühlmann,

In answer to your letter of 8 June, under cover of which you sent me the memorandum attached to AS. 2562,[1] I agree to support an application, made without the statement of any reasons, for 40 million marks to be placed at your disposal for the purpose in question.[2]

RÖDERN

[1] Document No. 133.

[2] It is doubtful whether these funds reached Moscow at all—they certainly did not get there before Mirbach was assassinated on 6 July. On 29 June Bussche telegraphed to Moscow (telegram No. 205, AS 2761 in Deutschland Nr. 131 secr, volume 18) in order to find out in which way the Minister in Moscow wanted the money transferred.

The first reply came from Riezler on 10 July, who asked for the July allocation of 3 million marks to be transferred to the account of the central commission of the Deutsche Bank (A 29400 in Deutschland 131 secr, volume 19). The second reply (telegram No. 599, AS 3462, in the same volume) was dispatched by Helfferich on 30 July, asking for the equivalent value in roubles to be put at his disposal by the Consulates-General in Petrograd and in Moscow. Helfferich, the successor of Mirbach, had little time in which to use this money. Discouraged by Mirbach's fate, Helfferich stayed in Moscow only ten days; during this time he ventured outside the Embassy building once. Finally, he fled from Moscow.

136

The Minister in Moscow to the State Secretary

AS 2936   25 June 1918

Dear Chief,

I should like to avail myself, today, of your invitation to write to you privately from time to time, in order briefly to sum up a few points about the situation here, which you might be quite pleased to have crystallized in a single letter, in spite of the fact that they are already to be found spread through various reports.

After two months' careful observation, I can now no longer give Bolshevism a favourable diagnosis. We are unquestionably standing by the bedside of a dangerously ill man, who might show apparent improvement from time to time, but who is lost in the long run.

Quite apart from the fact that Bolshevism would definitely soon, of its own accord, fall a victim to the process of internal disintegration which is devouring it, there are all too many elements working tirelessly to hurry its end as much as possible and to settle the succession favourably to their own designs.

One day we might therefore be faced with what for us would be the most undesirable state of affairs possible, i.e. Social Revolutionaries, financed by the Entente and equipped with Czechoslovak arms, quite openly leading a new Russia back into the ranks of our enemies. (Of course this is not so terrible from a military point of view, but politically and economically it could not possibly be less desirable.)

If we now accept that Bolshevism has reached the end of its powers, then I think that we should seek to ensure that we are in a position to fill the vacuum which will result from its disappearance with a régime which would be favourable to *our* designs and interests—and this does not necessarily mean the immediate restoration of the Monarchy.

The basic essentials exist. To some extent they are only latent, but they could be stimulated into more vigorous activity at any moment.

We have groups of interested parties of the most varied shades at our disposal. First of all, there are the Monarchists, in the narrower sense of the word, who probably deserve consideration as the only available firm king-post for any possible combination, but who are not to be recommended. In general they are too confused and too lazy, and they are fundamentally only interested in winning back their former secure and comfortable living-conditions with our help.

The nucleus of which we are thinking should be composed of moderates from the right wing, Octobrists and Kadets (these reaching as far to the left as possible), especially as such a combination would ensure that we had a large percentage of the influential men of the industrial and banking worlds serving our essential economic interests.

This bloc, which is already quite powerful as it stands, could be further strengthened and hardened if we could draw the Siberians into it—though this would indeed be our hardest problem. Then, even further vistas, based on the mineral resources of Siberia, would appear, and, in this connexion, I will just touch on a few wider, almost unlimited possibilities of de-velopment which point us to the far and farthest East.

In the event of a change of orientation here, we would not even have to apply a great deal of force, and we could, to some extent, keep up appearances in our relations with the Bolsheviks right to the last moment. The continual mismanagement here, and the equally continual violent blows being struck against our interests, could be used as a motive for a military advance at any time *we* chose; and any military advance made by us on any considerable scale—and it would not even have to be directed against the two capitals—would automatically lead to the fall of Bolshevism, after which, equally automatically, the new organs of government, which we would be holding in readiness and which would be entirely at our service, would step into the ensuing gap.

Of course, nothing can be had absolutely free: we shall have to pay some kind of price, if not immediately, then in the later course of developments. The friends whom we may then have here will certainly not blindly accept the map of Russia as it was drawn by the treaty of Brest-Litovsk. They may well have already sufficiently detached themselves spiritually from Poland, Lithuania, and Courland; even the permanent renunciation of Livonia will not come too hardly to them. On the other hand, the amputation of Estonia will arouse much more bitterness (because of Reval), while it has become a positive political axiom that the permanent separation of the Ukraine from the rest of Russia must be proclaimed as impossible. Those in Ger-many who invest the Ukraine with some permanent value to us will find it hard to accept the idea of allowing it to be re-stored to the rest of Russia; those who regard its separation as a war-time measure will have less difficulty in altering their mode of thought on this matter.

I am, of course, perfectly aware that I am only seeing one section of the overall picture of the world. Only those who have the whole of this picture before them and who know all the various inter-relationships can make decisions. Nevertheless, I felt both the wish and the need to describe the sector for which I am responsible, as I seem to see it.   MIRBACH

APPENDIX I

Memorandum by Dr. Helphand

A 8629 in WK 11c
secr, volume 5

9th March 1915[1]

Preparations for a Political Mass Strike in Russia.

Preparations are to be made for a political mass strike in Russia, to take place in spring, under the slogan 'Freedom and Peace'. The centre of the movement will be Petrograd, and within Petrograd, the Obnuhov, Putilov, and Baltic works. The strike is to halt railway communications between Petrograd and Warsaw and Moscow and Warsaw, and to immobilize the South-Western Railway. The railway strike will be principally conducted to affect the large centres with considerable labour forces, the railway workshops, &c. In order to widen the scope of the strike, as many railway bridges as possible will be blown up, as during the strike movement of 1904 and 1905.

Conference of Russian Socialist Leaders

The task can only be fulfilled under the leadership of the Russian Social Democrats. The radical wing of this party has already gone into action, but it is essential that they be joined by the moderate minority group. So far it has been mainly the radicals who have prevented unification. However, two weeks ago their leader, Lenin, himself threw open the question of unification with the minority. It should be possible to achieve unity on a compromise policy, based on the necessity of exploiting the weakening of the administrative apparatus inside the country brought about by the war, and thus to initiate positive action. It should be understood that the moderate group has always been more strongly influenced by the German Social Democrats, and amongst them the personal authority of some of the German and Austrian Social Democratic leaders could still achieve a great deal. After careful preliminary probing, it is essential that a congress of Russian Social Democratic leaders be arranged in Switzerland or in some other neutral country. The following should take part in such a congress: (1) The Social Democratic majority party; (2) the minority party; (3) the Jewish League; (4) the Ukrainian organization, Spilka; (5) the Polish Social Democratic party; (6) the Social Democratic Party of Poland [sic]; (7) the Lithuanian Social Democratic party; (8) the Finnish Social Democrats. The congress can only take place if unanimous decisions on starting immediate action against Tsarism can be assured beforehand.

[1] The memorandum is undated. It was registered in the journal of the Foreign Ministry on 9 March 1917.

The congress might have to be preceded by a discussion between the Russian Social Democratic majority and minority parties. Possible additions to the list of participants in the congress might be: (9) the Armenian party Dashnackzutiun; (10) Hindshak.

Apart from its enormous significance in terms of organization, the congress would also, by its decisions, have a tremendous effect on public opinion in France and England.

The Russian Social Revolutionaries

Separate negotiations must be held with the Russian Social Revolutionary party. Its members are more inclined to nationalism, and its influence on the workers is minimal. In Petrograd it only has a few followers in the Baltic works. For the purposes of a mass strike, it can safely be ignored. On the other hand, the peasants are its sphere, and, with them, it wields considerable influence through the medium of the primary school teachers.

Local Movements

At the same time as these preparations to create a basis for the organization of a mass strike, agitation must also be begun immediately. Through Bulgaria and Rumania communications can be established with Odessa, Nikolaiev, Sevastopol, Rostov (on the Don), Batum, and Baku. During the revolution, the Russian workers in these areas made local and occupational demands which were first granted, but later repudiated, and they have not abandoned these demands. Only two years ago there was a strike of sailors and dock-workers which brought these old wishes into the limelight once again. Agitation should be based on these points, and then also take a political direction. While a general strike could probably not be achieved in the Black Sea basin, it might be possible, in view of the current unemployment there, to arrange local strikes in Nikolaiev, in Rostov, and among certain trades in Odessa. Such strikes would take on symptomatic significance by disturbing the peace which descended on internal strife within the Tsarist Empire at the beginning of the war.

For this agitation to be carried out, the Russian seamen's organization, which, in recent years, had its base first in Constantinople and then in Alexandria, must be re-established, and it would now have to have its centre in Constanta or Galati. The fact that the towns on the Black Sea will be severely disturbed by the war at sea, will make them especially amenable to political agitation. A special effort must be made to ensure that, as in 1905, the revolutionary organizations, supported by the workers, gain control of the city administration, so that they can alleviate the misery of the poorer classes, who are suffering terribly from the war. This, too, would serve the purpose of giving a new impulse to the general revolutionary movement. Should a rising occur in Odessa, it could be supported by the Turkish navy.

The prospects of a mutiny in the Black Sea fleet cannot be assessed until closer contact has been established with Sevastopol.

In Baku and the region of the oil-fields a strike could be organized relatively easily. Moreover, it is important that a considerable proportion of the workers there are Tartars, that is, Moslems. If a strike occurs, attempts will be made to set fire to the naphtha wells and the oil depots, as in 1905. There would also be a possibility of organizing strikes in the mining district on the Donets, and conditions in the Urals, where the Socialist majority party has a strong following, are particularly favourable. Political strikes could easily be organized among the miners there, if a little money were available, for the population is extremely poor.

Siberia

Special attention should be devoted to Siberia. In Europe, it is only known as the land of exile, but throughout the great tracts of Siberia, along the railways and the rivers, lives a strong peasant class, proud and independent, which would be happiest completely undisturbed by the central government.

In the towns there are lively business circles and a layer of intellectuals, consisting of political exiles and others influenced by them. The Siberian constituencies send Socialist deputies to the Duma. During the revolutionary movement of 1905, the entire administration lay in the hands of the revolutionary committee. The administrative apparatus is extremely weak, and, now that it is felt that there is no danger threatening from Japan, the military organization has been reduced to a minimum. These conditions make it possible to set up several centres of activity in Siberia. At the same time, preparations should be made to allow the political exiles to escape to European Russia, which would be a purely financial problem. In this way, several thousand of the best agitators, who have important connexions and enjoy unlimited authority, could be directed to the centres of agitation mentioned above and to Petrograd. This measure could, of course, only be carried through by the Socialist organizations themselves, as only they have sufficient knowledge of the usefulness of individual personalities.

The more determinedly the Socialist organizations take their stand and the more their activities are co-ordinated, the more all these undertakings will develop and interlock. On the other hand, the undertakings themselves—and they should be taken in hand immediately for this reason, if for no other—will act as a spur to the nuclei of the Socialist parties and will encourage them to achieve unity.

Press Campaign

At the same time, the general trend of the undertakings must be emphasized inside the Russian Socialist parties by discussion in the press, in pamphlets, &c. Pamphlets in Russian can be published in Switzerland. A Russian newspaper, *Golos*, which is edited by several leaders of the Socialist minority party, is published in Paris, and, in spite of the exceptional circumstances in which it appears, it has maintained a completely objective attitude to the war. This paper will not be able to avoid taking part in a discussion of party tactics. The Swiss and Italian Socialist newspapers can also be called on to publish these comments, as can the Danish, the Dutch, the Swedish, and the American Socialist press. Internationally reputed German Socialist leaders could easily take part in this discussion.

A press campaign would have a considerable effect on the attitude of the neutral states, especially on Italy, and this effect would be transmitted to Socialist circles in France and England. Even an objective portrayal of the course of the war, which could only be given in England and France under the aegis of the Socialists, and even then only with great difficulty, would be of great value.

The Socialist press in Bulgaria and Rumania could easily be influenced to wage a lively struggle against Tsarism.

Since the centre for revolutionary agitation in Southern Russia will be Rumania, the attitude of the Rumanian daily press is important for this reason alone, and it is, of course, even more important in determining Rumania's own attitude to the war. The large Rumanian newspapers are all in the service of the Russians, and their financial obligations are supposed to be such as would be difficult to overcome. However, it would not be very difficult to organize a group of reputable journalists to publish a large, independent daily newspaper with an explicit policy of closer contact with Germany. As the Rumanian press is tuned to a Russian victory, it has lost a great deal of prestige as a result of the course of the war so far, whereas this new paper would win itself a public through its objective news reports. The development of events would concentrate public opinion on it more and more, and would even force the other newspapers to change their attitude.

Agitation in North America

The United States demand special attention. The enormous number of Jews and Slavs there represent a very receptive element for anti-Tsarist agitation, and both the Russian Social Democrats and the Jewish League have important contacts there. A few agitators must be sent out to make a tour of these areas. Besides making a personal appearance, they would stimulate the existing forces on the spot into energetic action, strengthen the organizations, reinforce the many Russian and Jewish press undertakings, and thus bring about the development of systematic activity.

In view of the many contacts with Russia which the millions of Russian *emigrés*, most of whom have only recently left their own country, must have, this could well be of great importance. Moreover, a movement among the Russian *emigrés* in America could not fail to have an effect on public opinion there. Agitators from among these circles could also be sent to Russia. In the present war, in which the future of the German nation is at stake, the German element, too, should become more active. A strong anti-Tsarist movement among the Russians and the Russian Jews in America would favour action by the Germans. A few German and Austrian Social Democratic speakers should be sent over.

The Growth of the Revolutionary Movement

Agitation in the neutral states will have powerful repercussions on agitation in Russia, and vice versa. Further developments depend, to a large extent, on the course of the war. The jubilant mood which reigned in Russia in the first few days has already sobered considerably. Tsarism needs quick victories, while it is, in fact, suffering bloody reverses. Even if the Russian army merely remains pinned to its present positions throughout the winter, there will be grave dissatisfaction throughout the country. This mass mood will be exploited, deepened, extended, and spread in all directions by the apparatus for agitation sketched above. Strikes here and there, the risings produced by distress and the increase in political agitation will all embarrass the Tsarist government. If it takes reprisals, this will result in growing bitterness: if it shows indulgence, this will be interpreted as a sign of weakness and fan the flames of the revolutionary movement even more. Ample experience of this was gained in 1904 and 1905. If, on the other hand, the Russian army suffers a severe reverse, then the movement opposing the government may quickly assume undreamt-of proportions. In any case, it can be assumed that a political mass strike will take place in the spring, if all available forces are mobilized according to the plan sketched above. If the mass strike grows to any considerable extent, the Tsarist régime will be forced to concentrate the military forces at its disposal inside Russia principally on Petrograd and Moscow. In addition, the government will need troops to protect railway communications. During the strike of December 1905, two regiments were needed merely to protect the line between Petrograd and Moscow. Only by these means was it possible to counter the repeated attempts made by the strikers to blow up the railway bridges near Tiver and in other places, and to throw the guards regiments, who alone were able to suppress the rising, into Moscow. Although the main preoccupation is to be the imminent railway strike in the West, efforts will also be made to start other railway strikes wherever possible. Even if this does not succeed everywhere, the Tsarist government will have to employ large military forces for the protection of bridges, stations, &c., and, at the same time, the administrative apparatus will be thrown into confusion and will begin to disintegrate.

The Peasant Movement and the Ukraine

As in 1905, the peasant movements may be an important accompanying phenomenon alongside the events outlined above. The conditions in which the peasants in Russia are living have not improved since then; on the contrary, they have deteriorated. In the eyes of the Russian peasants, the whole problem is one of land. The peasants will therefore bring manorial land under the plough again, and thus threaten the landowners.

The fundamental basis of the Russian peasant problem is, of course, the question of land ownership, but the solution of this question is also closely linked with the formation of co-operatives and of organizations granting credit at low interest, with school education, and with the taxation system and the administration of the state in general. In the Ukraine, all these factors combine to produce a demand for autonomy. As long as Tsarism maintains its domination, which, in the Ukraine, follows a policy of giving the land to the Muscovite aristocracy and protecting the great Muscovite landowners against the Ukrainian peasants with all available means, the peasants have no alternative but to rebel as soon as they realize that the power of the government is weakening or that the régime is in difficulties. One of the first tasks facing a Ukrainian government will be to establish law and order in place of the conditions of anarchy which resulted from the Muscovite régime, and, supported by the confidence of the Ukrainian people, it will easily achieve this end. The formation of an independent Ukraine will be seen both as a liberation from the Tsarist régime and as a salvation from the chaos of peasant unrest.

If there is peasant unrest in Central Russia—and the peasants of Greater Russia will certainly not remain quiet if the Ukrainian peasants rise close by them—then the Social Revolutionary party will also have to abandon its policy of inactivity. Through the medium of the primary school teachers this party has considerable influence among the peasants of Greater Russia, and it is authoritative among the Trudovniki, the peasants' Peoples' Party in the Duma. The attitude of the Russian Social Democrats to peasant unrest would emerge at once if the peasants decided to oppose Tsarism.

The Movement in Finland

Within this general movement, important activities could be undertaken in Finland. The Finnish parties are in an awkward position, for there are considerable Russian military forces in the country. On the other hand, the Finns do not simply want to be annexed by Sweden. But the Swedes do not want to annex Finland: they simply want to turn it into a buffer state, i.e. an independent state. The Swedish party is a small minority in Finland. Therefore attempts must be made, above all, to achieve an agreement between the Swedish government and the more powerful Finnish parties, amongst which the Social Democratic party is the most important. This could probably be achieved by the Swedes' guaranteeing the Finns the widest possible measure of autonomy and leaving it to them to decide to which group of states they wish to attach themselves. Once such an agreement is reached, preparations for a general rising in Finland can be made quietly and systematically. The Finnish Social Democrats have excellent organizations, similar to those of the German Social Democrats, at their disposal. The obstinate defence of its rights against Tsarist despotism has trained the whole Finnish people in discretion and silent co-operation, in which the difference of language also helps a great deal. All the preparations are to be made secretly until some considerable wave of strikes breaks out in Russia. This would be the moment for a general rising in Finland. Because of Finland's large area, the Tsarist government would be faced with the choice of breaking down the military forces at their disposal into small, independent units which could attack the various storm centres, or concentrating their forces on the most important administrative and strategic points, thus abandoning the country to the rebels. The former were the tactics used by the Tsarists to defeat the revolutionary movement of 1905. Numerous expeditionary forces were formed, both large and small, and their commanders were given complete military and civil powers. The plan was worked out in Petrograd by a special commission, on which sat members both of the General Staff and of the highest administrative bodies. The revolutionaries' executive was well informed about the work of this commission, but was not able to frustrate its plan. Nevertheless, it took the Tsarist government the whole strength of its army and a period of two years to quash the rising. If the Tsarist government were now to adopt the same course in Finland, the Swedish army would have to intervene to protect Finnish independence, for, while this course is probably the best way to quash a rising, it makes the army absolutely defenceless against the intervention of hostile forces. The Tsarist government will therefore probably decide for the second course and withdraw the army to the administrative centres, i.e. to the coast and the railway just behind. They may even destroy the railway links with Sweden. In practice, the Russians will then only dominate the coast of the Gulf of Bothnia. Masters of their own house, the rebels will then form a National Guard, as in 1904 and 1905, take defensive measures, and make other provisions to permit the Swedish troops entry, which may have been complicated by the destruction of the railways. Naturally, a great deal depends on the development of events in Petrograd.

The Finns could be of great service, even before the general rising. They could provide information about the numbers, the disposition and the movements of Russian troops in Finland, and about the movements of the Russian navy. They could set up a signal service for directing the activities of aircraft. (The Finnish custom of painting country houses, and especially their roofs, red would be useful in this. An unpainted section on a red roof would act as a land-mark.) They could also set up wireless telegraphy stations and make provisions for blowing up bridges and buildings. Above all, they could permit the Russian revolutionaries to communicate with Petrograd. Since the country is very large, is immediately adjacent to the Petrograd region, and has regular, hourly traffic to Petrograd, they could set up an information and transport service, in spite of the military occupation. Stores of arms could be built up, and arms, explosives, &c., smuggled across to Petrograd.

The Caucasus

At the time of the revolution, the Tsarist government for a long time practically ignored the Caucasus. As the Caucasus was not threatened from outside, they began by allowing anything that might happen there to happen. This state of affairs was allowed to reach the point where the government tolerated governors who were in open contact with the revolutionary committee to head the administration. They were certain that, once they had re-established their domination in Russia proper, they would be able to subdue the Caucasus once again, and in this they have been proved perfectly right. This time, however, because of the Russo-Turkish war, the situation is quite different. There is a possibility of the secession of the Caucasus, and the significance of a rising to the rear of the fighting armies needs no further explanation. However, in contrast to Finland, where a well-organized, general rising is possible, the movement in the Caucasus will always suffer from national divisions and party struggles. In the years of the revolution, it was the Georgians who emerged as the most forceful of the Caucasians.

At that time, with the support of the smallholders' masses, they gained complete control of the government of Kutai, setting up their own administration, law-courts, &c. However, it was not the separatists but the Social Democrats who headed this movement. Some of the Armenians fought in the ranks of the Social Democrats, while the rest grouped themselves around the Armenian nationalist parties, which had long ago abandoned their separatist tendencies. However, it must be realized that, after the disappointments of the revolution and in face of the war, the separatist tendencies have naturally gained in popularity.

The Tartar workers took part in the strikes. In general, the Tartar masses played a reactionary role; they allowed themselves to be incited against the Armenians by agents of the Petrograd government, and this resulted in bloody encounters between the two national elements. However, since the call for a holy war, the Tsarist government will no longer be able to rely openly on the support of the Moslem population. They will nevertheless secretly foster religious hatred, and will encourage the Armenians' fear of just this holy war. It is therefore essential that first of all everything possible be done on the Turkish side to make it clear to the Caucasian Moslems that it is in fact the achievement of the aims of their holy war which demands their close co-operation with their Christian neighbours in the struggle against Tsarism. An agreement must be made at once between the Young Turks and the Armenian parties in Turkey, which are identical with those in Russia. The details of this project, which will involve a variety of difficulties in its realization, do not fall within the scope of this memorandum. However, attention must be drawn to the fact that a determined attitude on the part of the Russian Social Democrats would have enormous effects on the activities of the Armenians and Georgians in the Caucasus. The Social Democrats could perhaps take control of the whole movement, and they would therefore certainly encourage the national parties to join in the struggle by their attitude. This is another reason why the conference of Russian Socialist party leaders suggested above is an urgent necessity.

A holy war, which has the power to produce large movements in Persia, Egypt, North Africa, &c., will hardly have much effect in Russia. The Tartars on the Volga and the Koma will certainly make no move, for they are a peaceful and completely subjugated people, who would face the opposition of the overwhelming numerical superiority of the Russian population. The situation in the Caucasus is slightly different, but one must realize that the Tartars there were pacified long ago. The memory of the heroic struggle for independence fought in the past has faded, and the Moslem population is not yet sufficiently civilized to begin a modern revolutionary movement. The old conflict between the Caucasian mountain tribes and the Russians was simply a fight against any kind of centralized state. Since then, the tribal organization has completely disintegrated. The tribal chiefs have become landowners; the contact between them and the masses is now only slight, and the people have lost their sense of independence. Because the Moslems feel economically and culturally inferior to the Christian population, they look to the government, as the most powerful among powerful forces, for support. They would certainly prefer a Moslem government, but such a government would first of all have to prove itself strong enough to defeat the Tsarist government. The Turkish army will be favourably received, but it will have to conquer the might of the Russians with the strength of its own arms. This does not, of course, entirely exclude the possibility of the formation of isolated rebel bands, especially on the Persian border. There is no prospect of a large-scale partisan war being waged by the Moslem population in the Caucasus. However, a rising of the Kuban cossacks is not beyond the realms of possibility, and Ukrainian propaganda could be useful in preparing such a rising.

The Culmination of the Movement

The growth of the revolutionary movement within the Tsarist Empire will, among other things, produce a state of general unrest. In addition to the effects of the general course of the war, special measures could be adopted to aggravate this unrest. For obvious reasons, the Black Sea basin and the Caucasian basin are the most favourable districts. Particular attention should be devoted to Nikolaiev, as the shipyards there are working at great pressure for the launching of two large warships. Efforts are to be made to start a strike among the workers there. This strike need not necessarily be political in character; it could just as well be based on the workers' economic demands.

It can be accepted as a fact that the Tsarist government needs quick victories to maintain itself. If it lasts until the spring, even the present situation, in which the Russian army is being systematically harried without achieving any progress, can only result in a revolution. However, the difficulties facing the movement must not be overlooked.

First and foremost, there is mobilization, which has stripped the country of its most active younger elements; and then there is also the growth of national feeling which has resulted from the war. However, in face of the failure of the war, this very feeling is bound to turn into bitterness and be directed against Tsarism. It must be realized that, unlike the Ukrainian or the Finnish Social Democrats, the Russian Social Democratic party will never adopt a position hostile to the Russian Empire. Even at the time of the revolution, this party included over a million workers within its organizations, and, since then, its following among the masses has increased to such an extent that the government has twice been forced to alter the electoral law, for fear of allowing the Duma to be flooded with Social Democratic deputies. Such a party must surely represent the interests and the moods of the masses, who did not want the war, and are now merely taking part in it. The Social Democrats are in determined opposition to the unlimited external extension of power which is the aim of Tsarist diplomacy. They see this as a severe obstacle to the internal development of the nations forming the Empire—including the Russian nation. They consider the Tsarist government responsible for this war, and will therefore hold it responsible for the futility and the failure of the war. They will demand the fall of the government and a quick conclusion of peace.

If the revolutionary movement achieves any considerable scale, and even if the Tsarist government is still in power in Petrograd, a provisional government can be set up to raise the question of an armistice and a peace treaty and to open diplomatic negotiations.

If the Tsarists should actually be forced to make an armistice before this occurs, then the better the revolutionary movement is prepared, the more violently it will break out then. Even if the Tsarist government succeeds in retaining power for the duration of the war, it will never be able to maintain itself after a peace dictated from abroad.

Thus the armies of the Central Powers and the revolutionary movement will shatter the colossal political centralization which is the embodiment of the Tsarist Empire and which will be a danger to world peace for as long as it is allowed to survive, and will conquer the stronghold of political reaction in Europe.

Siberia[1]

Particular attention should also be devoted to Siberia because the enormous deliveries of artillery and other arms from the United States to Russia will probably pass through Siberia. The Siberian project must therefore be treated separately from the rest. A few energetic and sufficiently equipped agents should be sent to Siberia on special missions to blow up the railway bridges. They would find a sufficient number of assistants among the exiles. Explosives would have to be provided from the mines in the Urals, but small quantities could probably be smuggled over from Finland. Technical instructions would have to be worked out here.

Press Campaign

The predictions made about Rumania and Bulgaria have been proved correct by the course of developments since the completion of this memorandum. The Bulgarian press is now completely pro-German, and there is a noticeable swing in the attitude of the Rumanian press. The provisions which we have made will soon show even better results. It is now of particular importance to begin work on [word missing].

1. Financial support for the majority group of the Russian Social Democrats, which is fighting the Tsarist government with all the means at its disposal. Its leaders are in Switzerland.

2. The setting up of direct communications with the revolutionary organizations in Odessa and Nikolaiev, via Bucharest and Jassy.

3. The creation of contacts with the Russian seamen's organization. Some contact has already been made through a gentleman in Sofia, and further contacts are possible via Amsterdam.

[1] The rest of the memorandum forms a separate unit. It was written on a different typewriter; it contains Helphand's afterthoughts.

4. Support for the activities of the Jewish Socialist organization, 'The League' (not Zionists).

5. Finding authoritative Russian Social Democratic and Social Revolutionary personalities in Switzerland, Italy, Copenhagen, and Stockholm and furthering the efforts of such of them as are determined on immediate and vigorous action against Tsarism.

6. Support for those Russian revolutionary writers who will continue to take part in the struggle against Czarism, even while the war is still on.

7. Connexions with the Finnish Social Democrats.

8. The organization of congresses of Russian revolutionaries.

9. Influencing public opinion in the neutral states, especially the opinions of the Socialist press and the Socialist organizations, favourably towards the struggle against Tsarism and towards connexions with the Central Powers. This has already been done successfully in Bulgaria and Rumania, but efforts to do so in Holland, Denmark, Sweden, Norway, Switzerland, and Italy must be continued.

10. The equipment of an expedition to Siberia, with the specific mission of blowing up the most important railway bridges and preventing the transport of arms from America to Russia. The expedition should also be provided with sufficient financial means to make it possible for a number of deported political prisoners to escape into the interior.

11. Technical preparations for a rising in Russia:

(a) Provision of accurate maps of the Russian railways, showing the most important bridges which must be destroyed if traffic is to be crippled, and also showing the main administrative buildings, depots, and workshops to which most attention should be devoted.

(b) Exact figures for the amount of explosives required to achieve the aim in every case. Here, consideration must be given to the shortage of materials and to the difficult circumstances in which the tasks will be carried out.

(c) Clear and simple instructions for the handling of explosives in blowing up bridges, blowing up large buildings, &c.

(d) Simple formulas for the preparation of explosives.

(e) Preparation of a plan for resistance to armed forces by the rebel population in Petrograd, including special consideration of the workers' quarters, the defence of houses and streets, the construction of barricades, and defence against cavalry and infiltrating infantry.

The Jewish Socialist 'League' in Russia is a revolutionary organization, supported by the workers, which gave considerable service even in 1904. It has nothing to do with the Zionists, from whom, by contrast, nothing can be expected:

1. Because their party structure is extremely loose.

2. Because a strong Russian patriotic trend has made itself felt in their ranks since the beginning of the war.

3. Because, after the Balkan War, the nucleus of their leadership actively sought to win the favour of English and Russian diplomatic circles—though this did not stop them from lobbying the German Imperial government as well.

4. Because they are incapable of any political action.

APPENDIX II

A Note on the Foreign Ministry, 1914–18

Since Bismarck's time, the Reichskanzler was also the Foreign Minister. He was assisted by a State Secretary, and first by one, later in the war by two Under State Secretaries.[1] Further down, the Foreign Ministry consisted of the following departments:

Abteilung Ia, which was concerned with matters of high policy, and also some personnel matters of officials in the diplomatic service.

Abteilung Ib, concerned with personnel matters, code and courier matters, court procedure, protocol and finance.

Abteilung II, concerned with trade and transport, also with medical, veterinary and quarantine matters, and railways, post, telegraph, &c.

Abteilung III was the legal department.

The missions and consulates abroad were a part of the Ministry. In 1914, before the outbreak of the war, there were 44 missions, of which 9 were Embassies.

This organization of the Ministry survived the war and was preserved till March 1920, when the Foreign Ministry of the Weimar Republic was radically reorganized. Though the outbreak of the war did not affect the structure of the Ministry, it lost most of its peacetime functions. Only the missions in the neutral countries remained. Most of these missions accommodated military Abwehr sections, subordinate to the High Command. Foreign Ministry officials often held military ranks, and their transfers from diplomatic to military service and vice versa were frequent.

The headquarters of the Auswärtiges Amt were in Berlin W. 8, Wilhelmstrasse Nos. 75 and 76. Since the General Headquarters became, in a sense, the political capital of the Empire, where the Kaiser lived, and the Chancellor and the State Secretary spent most of their time in the first months of the war, the Foreign Ministry sent two liaison officers there, one attached to the General Headquarters (Treutler 1914–16, Lersner 1916–18) and the other to the Imperial Court (Grünau). Later in the war, before the conclusion of the peace of Brest-Litovsk, a similar post was created at the Eastern Command.

[1] State Secretary: Dec. 1912–Nov. 1916, Jagow; Nov. 1916–Aug. 1917, Zimmermann; Aug. 1917–July 1918, Kühlmann; July 1918–Oct. 1918, Hintze.
Under State Secretary: May 1911–Nov. 1916, Zimmermann; U.St.S. I (Pol.) Nov. 1916–Oct. 1918 Stumm; U.St.S. II (Econ.) Oct. 1916–Dec. 1918, Bussche.

INDEX OF PROPER NAMES

PRINTED IN
GREAT BRITAIN
AT THE
UNIVERSITY PRESS
OXFORD
BY
CHARLES BATEY
PRINTER
TO THE
UNIVERSITY

DATE DUE

MAY 1 '64			
APR 9 '65			
SEP 10 '65			
GAYLORD			PRINTED IN U.S.A.